# TEACHING THE CORE SKILLS OF
# LISTENING & SPEAKING

# TEACHING THE CORE SKILLS OF
# LISTENING & SPEAKING

## ERIK PALMER

 Alexandria, VA USA

1703 N. Beauregard St. • Alexandria, VA 22311-1714 USA
Phone: 800-933-2723 or 703-578-9600 • Fax: 703-575-5400
Website: www.ascd.org • E-mail: member@ascd.org
Author guidelines: www.ascd.org/write

Gene R. Carter, *Executive Director;* Richard Papale, *Acting Chief Program Development Officer;* Stefani Roth, *Interim Publisher and Acquisitions Editor;* Julie Houtz, *Director, Book Editing & Production;* Katie Martin, *Editor;* Louise Bova, *Graphic Designer;* Mike Kalyan, *Production Manager;* Valerie Younkin, *Production Designer*

All material from the Common Core State Standards for English Language Arts & Literacy in History/Social Studies, Science, and Technical Subjects and from the Common Core State Standards for Mathematics © 2010 by the National Governors Association Center for Best Practices and Council of Chief State School Officers. All rights reserved.

All web links in this book are correct as of the publication date below but may have become inactive or otherwise modified since that time. If you notice a deactivated or changed link, please e-mail books@ascd.org with the words "Link Update" in the subject line. In your message, please specify the web link, the book title, and the page number on which the link appears.

PAPERBACK ISBN: 978-1-4166-1756-3     ASCD product # 114012     n3/14

Also available as an e-book (see Books in Print for the ISBNs).

Quantity discounts: 10–49 copies, 10%; 50+ copies, 15%; for 1,000 or more copies, call 800-933-2723, ext. 5634, or 703-575-5634. For desk copies: www.ascd.org/deskcopy

**Library of Congress Cataloging-in-Publication Data**
Palmer, Erik, 1953- author.
   Teaching the core skills of listening and speaking / Erik Palmer.
      p. cm.
   Includes bibliographical references and index.
   ISBN 978-1-4166-1756-3 (pbk. : alk. paper) 1. Oral communication–Study and teaching–United States. 2. Listening–Study and teaching–United States. 3. Language arts–United States. 4. Education–Standards–United States–States. I. Title.
   LB1572.P35 2014
   302.2242071–dc23
                                                             2013046269

23  22  21  20  19  18  17  16  15  14              1  2  3  4  5  6  7  8  9  10  11  12

# TEACHING THE CORE SKILLS OF LISTENING & SPEAKING

# ACKNOWLEDGMENTS

So I'm sitting in my office and the phone rings. It's Stefani Roth, an acquisitions editor for ASCD. She makes it clear that ASCD wants me to write a book for them. I explained that I had published two books with Stenhouse Publishers and I love the people there and what they have done for me. Stefani could not have been more understanding or more accommodating: "We will do whatever it takes to make you and them comfortable!" And she could not have been more insistent: "You are the only person who can write this book!" Thank you, Stefani, for promoting this project and for believing in me.

I also have to acknowledge, then, Holly Holland, my editor at Stenhouse, and Dan Tobin, the company president. While perhaps a bit disappointed that my next book was not going to be a Stenhouse book, they were supportive and more than willing to wish me well. Thank you both for your understanding and encouragement.

Only by getting input from a great editor can you discover the brilliant tweaks, suggestions, and additions that can dramatically improve your words. Katie Martin offered many insightful comments and helped me clarify many key concepts. As an author, I think it is great fun to find an improved way of saying something. So many times Katie provided that better way. Thank you, Katie.

I have to acknowledge, as always, my wife, Anne. She encouraged me to move from the classroom to a somewhat bigger stage. She puts up with the light going on in the middle of the night so I can write down an idea that's popped into my head. She celebrates all of the accomplishments, trivial and important. She holds down the fort while I am off speaking or leading workshops. Thank you, Anne. You help make many possibilities reality.

I also have to thank some people I don't know. First, I'd like to acknowledge the unknown person who heard me speak at some conference and excitedly communicated to the folks at ASCD that I had an important message that needed to be shared. Without that person, this whole process might never have started. And I'd like to thank you, the reader. It is your interest in what I have called "The Forgotten Language Arts" that will bring a renewed emphasis to these most important skills. The work that you do to develop listening and speaking skills will be the single greatest gift you give to your students, and this gift will last a lifetime.

# INTRODUCTION

*How do you teach listening and speaking?*

There are two ways to approach this question. The first is in a global, impersonal sense. The focus is procedure. Think of it as similar to questions such as "How do you copy a paragraph in a MS Word document?" and "How do you find a common denominator?" Many of us could quickly rattle off the process for finding a common denominator, but how many of us are prepared to describe the process for building strong oral communication? How *do* you teach listening and speaking?

My sense is that when many teachers consider the question, their first thought is, "Well, you really don't have to. Speaking? My kids are always talking! And teaching *listening*? We are *always* doing that—always reminding them to sit still and be quiet." But is this true? Are all of our students well spoken? Have they all mastered listening to each other, entertaining diverse points of view, evaluating evidence and supporting arguments, collaborating with others, and analyzing the media they are exposed to daily? Do they all communicate effectively in conversations, discussions, and presentations? Obviously not. Listening and speaking are skills, and like all skills, they can be improved significantly with deliberate instruction and purposeful practice.

1

The second way to respond to the question is personal: How do *you* teach listening and speaking? What do *you* do in your classroom to help students learn to listen and speak effectively?

Imagine you are in a faculty meeting, and your administrator stands up and explains that the school will be launching a listening and speaking skills initiative in line with new standards. "As part of your assessment this year," your administrator says, "I will look for specific lessons that teach to the listening and speaking standards."

Be honest, now: How prepared would you be?

If the new initiative had focused on writing standards, you'd probably be in good shape, especially if you teach elementary school or language arts. In those contexts, every teacher teaches writing and knows that there's more to "writing instruction" than simply "make students write." It's necessary to prepare specific lessons that teach students *how* to be better writers—lessons that break the skill of writing well into subcomponents. There are lessons and worksheets about capitalization, punctuation, and sentence structure. Students complete practice exercises focused on topic sentences and supporting details, good word choice, and effective organization.

Yet when the topic turns to listening and speaking, how many of us can break oral communication skills into subcomponents? How many of us can point to specific lessons? Yes, we incorporate oral activities into our instruction. Our students listen to lectures, explanations, and material read aloud. They ask questions, speak in small groups, and present reports on various topics. But just as making students write a lot doesn't automatically make them good writers, making students listen a lot does not automatically make them good listeners. And occasionally making them speak in front of the class does not automatically make them good speakers.

## Challenging Current Practice

When I ask teachers at workshops how they teach speaking, these are the kinds of answers I get:

Our 7th grade students do a history project, and they have to dress up like a historical figure and do a seven-minute presentation in front of the class and parents. Other students listen and give feedback.

We record a podcast about our favorite activities and post it on the class wiki where students can post comments.

Students have a weekly Share Time, and they take turns talking about the item they bring in. The class asks questions.

I do "Ignite" presentations about our project-based learning topics.

After the poetry unit, we have a "Poetry Café," and each student memorizes and presents a poem to the class. The students vote on the best poem.

The students take turns doing "Science in the News," an oral report about scientific events that are making headlines. I have students discuss the events.

What you see here is a nice sampling of the kinds of listening and speaking activities that go on, formally and informally, at all grade levels and in all subjects. However, none of these responses actually answers the question I asked: "How do you *teach* listening and speaking?" These teachers do not distinguish oral communication *activities* from oral communication *instruction*. It's a very common mistake—and one that must be challenged. To the Poetry Café teacher, I might say the following:

Yes, you require every student to recite a poem and require the class to listen, but do you teach specific lessons first? For instance, poetry will only come alive if the poems are well delivered. Do you have lessons about vocal inflection, what it is, how it affects meaning, and how it sustains interest? Do you make it clear to students that the speaker must add life to the words and the audience must listen for it? Do you have lessons focused on pacing, pausing, and adjusting speed for effect so that your students will be able to use each of these techniques to enrich their presentation? Do you ask listeners to be aware of the techniques used?

I might challenge the teacher who assigns "Science in the News" this way:

How do you prepare your students for these oral reports? Do you have lessons on eliminating "like," "ya know," and similar phrases? Do you have lessons on effective volume and pronunciation to ensure that every word is heard? How do you prepare your students to discuss these news stories? Do you teach them to ask questions for elaboration? Do you teach them to analyze and evaluate the speaker's motives—to ask, for example, why the speaker chose this article, "Hottest July in History," as newsworthy and not some other topic?

In all likelihood, few students assigned to recite a poem receive the kind of lessons I've described, and few students discussing content-area topics, current events, and project work get the sort of guidance I have mentioned. Although their teachers might make comments on such matters *after* the presentations, only a very small number offer direct instruction *before*. I know that for part of my teaching career, the answer to "How do *you* teach listening and speaking?" was "Well, I guess I really don't." I suspect the same is true for many other teachers. And it might be true for you.

This book is designed to change that—and to help you answer the "How do you teach listening and speaking?" question in both the general and the personal sense. Together, we will look at the importance of listening and speaking skills—whether for conversing one-to-one, engaging in a small-group discussion, participating in a meeting or webinar, delivering or consuming a podcast, making a major presentation, or learning online—and consider specific ways that *you* might teach listening and speaking.

## Listening and Speaking: "Core" Skills

So why this focus on listening and speaking? Why now?

The immediate impetus may be the Common Core State Standards. As I write this, most U.S. states have adopted the standards, and the Common Core's set of English Language Arts and Literacy (ELA) standards include "Speaking and Listening" as one of four content strands, alongside reading, writing, and language (grammar and usage). I will talk much more about the standards in later chapters. And I will say outright that I am happy that after decades of oral communication being an afterthought (if not ignored completely), it is getting attention.

I have structured this book to align with the six Common Core anchor standards for speaking and listening. Although I am aware that the Common Core may one day disappear and be replaced by a newer educational initiative, I believe the concepts these standards address—skills that all parents would see as appropriate and necessary for their child to learn—have enduring value and are a sound foundation for oral communication instruction.

Consider too, that the Common Core State Standards reflect the movement toward improved college and career readiness. Ask yourself, what skills are most useful in the world beyond our K–12 classrooms? What will our graduates be doing, and what must they all be able to do successfully, no matter what field they are in? I would argue that the answer is *communicate*. And what does communicating in the workplace entail? Take a look at these numbers (Worth, 2004, p. 3):

**How We Spend Our Communication Time**

| | |
|---|---|
| Writing: | 9% |
| Reading: | 16% |
| Talking: | 30% |
| Listening: | 45% |

As adults on the job, we devote fully three-fourths of our communication to listening and speaking. I believe that alone is justification for increasing efforts to prepare students to listen and speak well, but I will offer additional justification as we explore these skills.

## Changing Our Teaching

As I said, few of us have a firm idea of how to teach listening and speaking. This is not surprising. Our teacher preparation included classes about how to teach writing, reading, math, and science. We took classes on discipline and classroom control and on how to work with diverse learners and learners with special needs. In our teaching practice, we have professional development focused on differentiation, response to intervention (RTI), bully proofing, and using technology. Is there anything about how to teach oral communication skills, either in pre-service or in-service training? No.

Successfully teaching listening and speaking is a matter of both rethinking what we do and redefining our expectations of students. For example:

• Parroting back information does not signify good listening or good speaking.

• Quietly waiting for the chance to give an opinion without considering what anyone else is saying is not acceptable.

• Watching hours of video without being able to critique the techniques used to produce the video is problematic.

• One-way presentations in which a teacher or student talks *at* the class without the class thinking about and analyzing the presentation should not be allowed.

• Assigning speeches before students have learned the specific skills needed to give a good speech is unfair.

• Making podcasts without having first honed the communication skills involved and then posting the resultant poor speaking on the class webpage or YouTube is an embarrassment.

In short, this book is about taking something we all "sort of" address and making our instruction much more purposeful, directed, and specific. I will examine the expectations in the Common Core's Speaking and Listening standards and suggest ways to help students meet these standards. They are more wide-ranging than the words *listening* and *speaking* suggest and, again, they would have broad value even if there were no such thing as the standards movement. While some teachers may be masters at fostering the targeted, standards-based skills—collaborative discussion, evidence-based argumentation, valid reasoning, and so on—for many, teaching this content presents new challenges. For them, I offer activities associated with each skill, targeted to a variety of grade levels.

Finally, this book is intended to motivate you. As the examples in the chapters ahead illustrate, speaking and listening skills cross all content areas, and they are tied to long-term student success. For a long time now, instruction has focused heavily on the subjects addressed in state-mandated tests, and because listening and speaking were left off "the big test," they have not received the instructional emphasis they deserve. That has to change, and it *is* changing—due to new standards focused on college and career readiness and the reality of 21st century communication. It's time to teach listening and speaking. Let's get started.

# 1

## THE MOST FUNDAMENTAL SKILLS FOR SUCCESS

The cliché is that if you asked a fish about water, the fish would reply, "What's water?" Completely surrounded it, the fish doesn't even recognize water as a separate entity and certainly doesn't realize water's importance.

This is how it is with listening and speaking. They are so deeply embedded in so many aspects of our lives that most of us don't think about them much. Like the fish with water, we take listening and speaking for granted. It's time to change that—to bring listening and speaking to the forefront of educators' minds and to purposefully teach the listening and speaking skills that are the foundation of so much of human interaction.

This is probably the right time to mention that, yes, I prefer the phrase "listening and speaking" to the "speaking and listening" that's more common in English language arts standards and discussions of those standards. And the reason I turn the phrase around is to emphasize that in life and in all learning, listening is the predominant language art.

## Listening Comes First

How do infants learn? What is their first exposure to language? Listening. We all listened before we spoke and well before we read or wrote. Even our most visual and kinesthetic students have a learning history that began with listening. Appendix A to the Common Core ELA/Literacy standards examines the crucial connection between listening and learning. One of the references is to a study by Sticht and James, who "found evidence strongly suggesting that children's listening comprehension outpaces reading comprehension until the middle school years" (Common Core State Standards Initiative [CCSSI], 2010b, p. 26). In other words, all of us were auditory learners once, and all of our young students will gain more from listening than from any other input.

Even after reading comprehension catches up and students are able to effectively get information from print, they still take in a tremendous amount of information from listening—to their teachers, of course, but also to one another and to speech delivered via various electronic media. The International Listening Association claims that 85 percent of a student's learning is derived from listening (Mackay, 2005). It would be a challenge to find a teacher who *doesn't* believe that we can improve student learning by teaching them to listen well.

## Listening + Speech = Classroom Communication

If listening is the primary way that students take in information, it makes sense to pay close attention to what they're listening *to*. In the classroom, it's most likely to be spoken language—lectures, certainly, but also process explanations, project instructions, one-on-one conferences, presentations given by classmates, and discussions in groups. Education is fundamentally and unquestionably grounded in oral communication.

Studies reveal that students spend 50 to 75 percent of classroom time listening to teachers, other students, and audio media (Bass, 2005). Teachers lecture, explain, and cajole. We answer questions, present, and lead discussions. Most of our important directions, announcements, and explanations are oral. Given that so much teacher time is spent speaking, it would be wise to figure out how to do it well. And when the teacher is not talking, students still spend time listening—to other students as they present, to videos shown, to each other as they work together. You have heard many student discussion comments and probably hundreds of student presentations. How many were impressive? Would learning improve in your classrooms if those comments and presentations were well spoken?

Oral language dominates even outside of traditional instructional approaches. Some might point to the flipped classroom as an exception, but this model doesn't reduce the amount of listening students do; it just moves listening to the home. In fact, flipped instruction absolutely requires that the teacher command impressive oral communication skills. It is difficult to make a riveting presentation for a 10-inch screen. Requiring students to watch much of what teachers are currently putting out there amounts to cruel and unusual punishment (Palmer, 2012).

It's no different with online instruction. In my state, Colorado, a student in a rural high school who would otherwise not have access to AP Physics can now link up to an AP Physics classroom hundreds of miles away. But in order to do well in this environment, the online learner needs strong independent listening and media literacy skills, and she needs her faraway AP Physics teacher to have strong speaking and media presentation skills.

With so much of learning based on listening, we have to make sure that both the listeners and the speakers being listened to are competent. Let me be clear: I don't want my emphasis on listening and speaking as the core skills of language arts to devalue the work of reading teachers or discourage the teaching of writing. We and our students certainly read and write to learn, and we must make our students competent readers and writers. But think about *how* we teach reading and writing. Think about how much listening and speaking is involved. The water is everywhere, and everything depends upon it.

Now let's get more specific and look at the crucial roles listening and speaking play across content areas.

## Listening and Speaking in Classroom Discussion

Every class has discussions. I think it's because, intuitively, we are aware that discussions enhance understanding. As students verbalize and listen to others, they can gain insights and learn more about the subject under discussion, whether it's a poem, a function in calculus, a tectonic plate in geography, or an amendment to the Constitution.

There is an established connection between discussions and academic achievement. In one study, inserting a 10-minute discussion of a story during a 90-minute language arts class had a significant impact on students' performance, improving their grasp of the story's basic facts, of the characters' feelings and motives, and of the story's overall meaning (Fall, Webb, & Chudowsky, 1997). When students discuss, they are more likely to retain the information and be able to retrieve it later (Hammond & Nessel, 2011). Discussions also improve intellectual agility and help develop skills of synthesis and integration (Brookfield & Preskill, 1999). All the benefits of discussion are enhanced when the discussion participants are skilled speakers and listeners.

## Listening and Speaking in Reading Instruction

When I started teaching, my teammates told me that they all required one traditional, stand-up-and-speak book report every quarter. I was quite sure they meant that I should be doing the same, so that's what I did. It was only after many, many boring student book report talks that I started to wonder what the point of this assignment was. Was it to see if my students understood the books they read? If that's what I really wanted to find out, I could just ask them to tell me about the book in writing or in a personal conference. Was the goal to "scare" students into reading? "You'd better read, because otherwise you will look foolish when you have to give a talk in front of the whole class." No, that wasn't it. (And if it had been, I would've needed to rethink my ideas about student motivation.) Was I hoping these talks would inspire other students to read the books their classmates described? That was closer to what I had in mind. But apparently I needed to teach my students to speak about these books in a way that could inspire, because I wasn't seeing anybody sprinting to the library at the end of class. Actually, if the assignment really *was* about oral presentation, shouldn't I be giving my students instruction on how to present well? Why was I just assuming they all knew what to do?

Why *do* teachers assign oral book reports? I am surprised at how often I get quizzical looks when I ask this question. First, yes, we want to encourage reading. Students get better at something when they have more opportunities to practice it, and requiring one book report a quarter provides regular reading practice. Book reports also prompt readers to think critically about what they are reading in order to present the main character's traits and how she changed during the book, to describe the plot points and climax, to discuss the themes, and so on. But students could demonstrate this kind of critical thinking in other ways. Implicit in assigning book reports, then, is that we want to involve both the presenter and the listeners in this critical thinking. We want to encourage both the presenter and the listeners to read this book and other books. That means the speaker has to have strong presentation skills. And that means we need to teach those skills.

Oral book reports were not the only listening and speaking practices incorporated into my reading instruction. I read aloud to students, another familiar and seldom-questioned feature of many classrooms. The rationale for this one is easier to convey. We read aloud to demonstrate the enjoyment of reading but also to expose our students to language and to ways of using language that they would not otherwise encounter. Well-chosen stories are a way to introduce new words and their proper pronunciation in an engaging, memorable context. Himmele and Himmele (2012) put it this way:

> In addition to getting kids hooked on books, narrative read-alouds are an effortless way to help students acquire the academic language they will need to comprehend informational texts... research has shown a strong positive correlation between read-aloud experiences and vocabulary development. (¶4–5)

Certainly another benefit of reading aloud is that it shows students how words on a page (or screen) can come to life and become something meaningful and valuable. When a teacher models good reading, complete with inflection, expression, gestures, and explanations, individual words combine to form a big picture and become a way to learn about other people and places—a doorway to adventure and understanding. In this data-driven era, we don't *measure* the value of instilling a love of literature in children, but the value is still there. Many struggling readers have been inspired to continue the struggle because some oral presentation made a story come alive. This only happens if the material is read well and if the students are listening well.

Why do we have students read aloud? The usual answer that we want to help them improve their reading fluency. Beginning readers are "word bound," focused on making sense of letters and letter combinations. At some point, they achieve fluency, meaning that the struggle to sound out words transitions to making sense of word combinations and getting meaning from print. Advanced readers move beyond fluency and begin to understand prosody, the rhythm and inflection in the writing. Orthographic clues such as italics, exclamation points, and bold print give readers suggestions about what the passage is supposed to *sound* like. But fluency and prosody in reading make no sense to children if there is no fluency or inflection in their speaking. How can students make their reading come alive if they have never been taught how to make their voice come alive? Until we teach oral language, we risk embarrassing student readers and boring student listeners.

Let's look at one more common feature of reading instruction: reader's theater. Why do we use it? Erika, an 8th grade language arts teacher in Denver, offers this explanation in a video she made for the online book *Digitally Speaking*:

It helps the students see that literature can come alive. Using your voice to portray the actors and the characters helps the students see that it's not just boring words on a page. It's exciting information that can relate to what they are doing today. Practicing speaking skills is really important so that when we do reader's theater, the student can really get into the part of the character.... It's about using your voice and using life in your voice to bring the characters to life and to further understand why the characters think what they think or do what they do or say what they say. (Palmer, 2012)

It is much easier to comprehend text when we practice it and speak it; it is easier to comprehend character motivation when we "become" the character and interact with other characters. What Erika points out is that successful reader's theater depends on successful speaking skills.

## Listening and Speaking in Writing Instruction

Sharon teaches 5th grade language arts. Like many English teachers, she frequently gives her students prompts that they respond to, in writing, in their journals. Afterward, she draws from the deck of student name-cards and asks individual students to share something they have written. They can share any piece of the writing they choose, and they can choose the selection for any reason. Other students are encouraged to chime in with comments. Step inside the classroom, and this is what you might hear:

*Jamal:* I like how I described something my sister said, because it's funny: "If you wasn't faster, he'd a done some damage."

*Sharon (the teacher):* I like the way you captured the way people really speak sometimes, Jamal. You have a good ear. What did others think?

*Kim:* Don't you have to write it better? That's bad English, isn't it?

*Sharon:* Well, it's not formal English, but sometimes we don't speak formal English. If you are quoting someone, you should record exactly what they say. How would you make it formal English if you wanted to?

*Andre:* I'd say, "If you weren't faster, he would of done some damage."

*Sharon:* "He would *of* done some damage?"

*Melissa: Have!* He would *have* done some damage!

Sharon has students listen to their classmates' writing as an opening to instruction, and she uses shared writing as a way to inspire students to improve, like so:

*Herschel:* I want to share this one part—"The cat was curled up and cozy just catching a few Zs." I wrote it like that because you told us to try alliteration.

*Sharon:* "Curled up and cozy!" That really works, doesn't it? Who has cats? Can't you just picture that? Very nice.

Herschel gets validated as a writer, and other students see an effective application of a concept presented in class. Sharon encourages students to "steal from one another and use others' good ideas." (The plagiarism lecture comes later—right now she wants students to copy good models.)

This is one way that teachers use listening and speaking in writing instruction. Peer conferences are another. As a student speaks his written words, he can often discover a mistake: a left-out word, an awkward phrase, a wrong-sounding verb tense, and so on. As the peer listens, she can notice those places where the writing is unclear or lacks detail. If she gives good comments, the writer gains information that can support better self-assessment and better writing in the future.

There is an obvious connection between writing and oral presentation. Skills overlap. A person writing an essay and a person writing a speech both need to identify the audience and craft a message for that audience. They both need to define a purpose, add interesting and relevant content, organize that content, use transitions, and craft a powerful conclusion. Oral assignments give us opportunities to reinforce what we teach in written assignments.

There is a side benefit as well: speaking assignments can encourage students to write. We have all heard that one of the most prevalent fears people have is a fear of public speaking. What we usually miss is that there are some people who *love* speaking. Some of your students hate writing, but when given an opportunity to talk, they will enthusiastically write to prepare for the activity they feel comfortable doing (Palmer, 2012). For these students, oral assignments become a way to get written language assignments without a battle. When the writing will lead to a podcast posted on the class wiki page rather than just another paper to hand to the teacher, their engagement increases exponentially.

## Listening and Speaking in Presentations

In math class, a student goes to the board to explain a solution to a problem. In science, lab partners explain their lab results to the entire class. In social studies, students do a newscast on a current political campaign. In health class, a team reports on smoking and its health effects. In French class, a student talks about the customary foods of France. In every subject, at some point we call upon students to convey information orally.

My experience is that those presentations are tolerated by classmates, and the general mediocrity of these presentations is tolerated by teachers. Although learning to tolerate mediocrity may be a life skill we (unfortunately) need to develop, this is not likely the goal teachers have in mind for these assignments. What they want is for these presentations to impart useful information, to further understanding, and to engage the whole class. If students possess effective listening and speaking skills, these aims are well within reach.

Early in my teaching career, my father gave me a copy of *Writing to Learn* by William Zinsser. I have always used writing as way to learn: if I write something down, the act of writing seems to help me remember. Zinsser makes a bigger claim, though—that information that is difficult to grasp becomes understandable through the process of writing. As the writer is forced to condense material into clear, logical, and accurate sentences, that material becomes part of the writer's knowledge. As Zinsser puts it, "The hard part isn't the writing; the hard part is the thinking" (1988, p. 56). It's a strong argument for writing across the curriculum. Writing in English class may be about creating effective topic sentences, but in other classes it is about making the content personally meaningful. Presenting orally requires the same kind of thinking that writing does. The act of creating a presentation helps the presenter, who gains a deeper understanding of the material. The learning sticks. No matter the content area, presenting-to-learn is an important strategy.

## Listening and Speaking as 21st Century Skills

Years ago, I heard a speaker say that my students could expect to spend half of their time on the job reading in order to keep up with the continual changes affecting the other half of their jobs. I believe that statement can be updated: when our students enter the workforce, they will be spending half of their time *listening*—to videos, webinars, and video conferences. This won't be the case only in high tech or professional careers, either. When I last got my hair cut, the stylist told me she had just finished a session of mandatory webinar training. In short, many of our students will find that professional success depends on having good listening skills.

The Partnership for 21st Century Skills, a national U.S.–based advocacy group focused on technology infusion in education, stresses that students must be proficient communicators, creators, critical thinkers, and collaborators. When we consider the digital tools created in the past 20 years, the demand for these "Four Cs" makes perfect sense. Podcasts, videos, webinars, FaceTime, and video conferences make it easy to collaborate, and communication skills are necessary to make that collaboration work.

The rise of online video presents a particularly powerful argument for the importance of oral communication. Chris Anderson, curator of the popular online TED talks, notes that the ease of making videos translates into easier transmission of information. Rather than trying to write about a procedure, for example, we can simply record video and let the viewer *hear* and *see* the procedure. As a result, writing is increasingly giving way to telling and to showing. Here's Anderson:

> I believe that the arrival of free online video may turn out to be just as significant a media development as the arrival of print. It is creating new global communities, granting their members both the means and the motivation to step up their skills and broaden their imaginations. It is unleashing an unprecedented wave of innovation in thousands of different disciplines: some trivial, some niche in the extreme, some central to solving humanity's problems. In short, it is boosting the net sum of global talent. (2010, ¶10)

Anderson has noticed that the motivation to step up skills extends to oral communication skills. When people see his TED talks online and listen to the expert speakers, they realize the need to become better speakers themselves. In other words, TED talks not only demonstrate how much good speakers can teach us via presentation, they also demonstrate the importance of effective oral language. Listeners are inspired by the innovative ideas in the talks, and they are also inspired to work on presenting their own ideas more effectively. And of course, the crowd-accelerated innovation Anderson talks about only occurs when listeners are effective at grasping the ideas and advancing them.

## Listening and Speaking in Language Acquisition

How did we learn our native language? Immersion. Long before we received any formal instruction, we picked up our native language first by hearing it spoken in natural and meaningful contexts and then by trying to use it ourselves (Weaver, 1980). In the same way, school-age children acquiring a new language need to experience how that language works, which involves understanding the interconnection among listening, speaking, reading, and writing. Language proficiency increases when we teach strategies that develop these interconnections (Shaw, 2008). We learned our first language by interacting with others, and to learn a new language, students need opportunities to use that language in meaningful interactions with others (Shrum & Glisan, 2000). Those interactions are primarily verbal.

Recall that vocabulary acquisition is one of the skills promoted by reading aloud. We find a similar situation in second-language instruction. Students participating in a textbook dialog exercise have a better chance of retaining new vocabulary words if they and their peers deliver the dialog well. The way words are spoken gives clues about their meaning. Proper inflection can reinforce that meaning. To do this presupposes that the students speak well in their native language. Dialog containing "It is hilarious!" will likely not be delivered well if the native language phrase "Que era de risa!" is not delivered well. By developing speaking skills in the first language, then, we can support second-language acquisition. When oral communication skills are strong, dialogue comes alive, retention is improved, the patterns of the target language are more easily detected, and interest and engagement are increased.

## Listening and Speaking in Instruction for Students with Disabilities

Consider these sobering statistics from the National Council on Disability (2004): more than 40 percent of U.S. secondary-age students with disabilities do not attain a high school diploma at the end of high school, and dropout rates for youth with disabilities are three to four times higher than for students without disabilities. To what extent does this reflect the failure of one-size-fits-all instruction to meet the needs of these students?

Universal Design for Learning (UDL) is a promising avenue for ensuring that *every* student in our schools can access content and demonstrate understanding. UDL takes its cue from the universal design movement in architecture—the idea of which was to make physical environments accessible for everyone. The classic example is the curb cut: equally beneficial to people in wheelchairs, parents pushing strollers, cyclists, delivery people with hand trucks, individuals with mobility issues, and your run-of-the-mill pedestrian.

UDL is guided by three principles:

*Principle I: Provide Multiple Means of Representation*
Learners differ in the ways that they perceive and comprehend information that is presented to them. For example, those with sensory disabilities (e.g., blindness or deafness); learning disabilities (e.g., dyslexia); language or cultural differences; and so forth may all require *different ways* of approaching content. Others may simply grasp information quicker or more efficiently through visual or *auditory* means rather than printed text.

*Principle II: Provide Multiple Means of Action and Expression*
Learners differ in the ways that they can navigate a learning environment and express what they know. For example, individuals with significant movement impairments (e.g., cerebral palsy), those who struggle with strategic and organizational abilities (executive function disorders), those who have language barriers, and so forth approach learning tasks very differently. Some may be able to *express themselves well in written text but not speech, and vice versa....*

*Principle III: Provide Multiple Means of Engagement*
Affect represents a crucial element to learning, and learners differ markedly in the ways in which they can be engaged or motivated to learn.... Some learners are highly engaged by spontaneity and novelty while others are disengaged, even frightened, by those aspects, preferring strict routine. Some learners might like to work alone, while others prefer to work with their peers. In reality, there is not one means of engagement that will be optimal for all learners in all contexts; providing *multiple options* for engagement is essential. (CAST, 2011, p. 5) [emphasis added]

How do the principles of UDL connect to the topic of this book? High-stakes testing has had the effect of focusing instructional intention on reading and writing (assessed subjects). UDL reminds us to consider how else students might access content and demonstrate understanding: by listening to the text rather than reading it, by recording a presentation rather than word processing a written report, or by reading and discussing with a partner instead of reading and reflecting alone. Our schools adequately address the strong reader and the strong writer; following the principles of UDL will help us address the strong listener and the strong speaker at the same time that we use listening and speaking to accommodate students with unique needs.

## Listening and Speaking in Life Beyond School

Business leaders have long recognized the need for effective communication in the workforce. Figure 1.1 shows employers' ratings of their "most-valued" skills, as identified on a 2012 survey conducted by the National Association of Colleges and Employers. Notice how many involve listening and speaking. Facility with written language barely makes the top 10.

| Figure 1.1 | The Top 10 Candidate Skills and Qualities Employers Seek |
|---|---|

1. Ability to verbally communicate with persons inside and outside the organization
2. Ability to work in a team structure
3. Ability to make decisions and solve problems
4. Ability to plan, organize, and prioritize work
5. Ability to obtain and process information
6. Ability to analyze quantitative data
7. Technical knowledge related to the job
8. Proficiency with computer software programs
9. Ability to create and/or edit written reports
10. Ability to sell or influence others

*Source:* National Association of Colleges and Employers (2012).

According to a Stanford Business School study, our students will graduate into a business world in which verbal fluency and sociability are the two most important predictors of success. (Cain, 2012). A senior manager at Eastman Kodak puts it this way: "It's not enough to be able to sit at your computer excited about a fantastic regression analysis if you're squeamish about presenting those results to an executive group" (Cain, 2012, p. 31). And, to be clear, we aren't talking about fear of large-group presentation only. Presenting those results may involve a small group and may not be in person but online. Success is likely to depend on being comfortable communicating orally in many different modes—in large-group presentations but also in small-group meetings, in person but also online.

Students graduate to civic responsibilities as well. I finished my teaching career as a civics teacher. Civics is a subject that naturally leads to many discussions of polarizing topics: the national debt, entitlements, gay rights, gun control, use of drones, and climate change to name a few. It is difficult to find models for civil and collaborative discussions of these issues. What we tend to see on television are less discussion than they are virulent attacks, which make for great theater and seem to attract viewers, but do nothing to move participants toward understanding and solution. Somewhere, this trend has to be reversed, and that somewhere may be your class as you teach listening and speaking skills: how to identify key points, how to construct counterarguments, how to reach evidence-supported conclusions, and so on.

In conclusion, listening and speaking are the water that surrounds everything in our classes and upon which instruction depends. We do a disservice to our students if we assume they can somehow become effective listeners and communicators without direct instruction.

We have all noticed the problem. Few teachers would say, "Not *my* kids! They have mastered listening and speaking!" We have all noticed the problem; now we need to respond to it. Effort is involved. Changing our teaching is involved. You may be tempted to view the next chapters as "More Work for Me." To some extent, they are. But I hope you also see what follows as "Essential Instruction That All Children Need." Let's get to it!

# 2

# CORE SKILLS, CORE STANDARDS

I debated about how closely I wanted to link this book to the Common Core State Standards for Speaking and Listening. As I have mentioned, some states have not adopted the Common Core, and some of the states that have are now backing out of the testing portion. The Common Core is a reality today, but eventually the entire movement will doubtless be replaced by "The Next Thing."

What ultimately convinced me to address the Common Core's listening and speaking standards directly is that they really do address core skills that will benefit all students for all time:

> The [Common Core's] Speaking and Listening standards require students to develop a range of broadly useful oral communication and interpersonal skills. Students must learn to work together, express and listen carefully to ideas, integrate information from oral, visual, quantitative, and media sources, evaluate what they hear, use media and visual displays strategically to help achieve communicative purposes, and adapt speech to content and task. (CCSSI, 2010a, p. 8)

What's more, each of the Common Core standards focused on listening and speaking is written in a way that presents a useful guide for scaffolding instruction. In this short chapter, we'll look at the structure of these standards and how they fit together to guide teaching and learning.

## The Standards' Structure

The Common Core State Standards are an attempt to articulate the proficiencies needed to be a "college- and career-ready" graduate. With that end in mind, the ELA/Literacy standards begin each section—reading, writing, speaking and listening, and language—with College and Career Readiness Anchor Standards. These are broad statements of the skills we want students to master. Grade-specific standards follow the anchor standards to provide specificity.

There are six anchor standards for speaking and listening, grouped under two topic headings—"Comprehension and Collaboration" (generally related to listening) and "Presentation of Knowledge and Ideas" (generally related to speaking). Here they are:

**Comprehension and Collaboration**
1. Prepare for and participate effectively in a range of conversations and collaborations with diverse partners, building on others' ideas and expressing their own clearly and persuasively.
2. Integrate and evaluate information presented in diverse media and formats, including visually, quantitatively, and orally.
3. Evaluate a speaker's point of view, reasoning, and use of evidence and rhetoric.

**Presentation of Knowledge and Ideas**
4. Present information, findings, and supporting evidence such that listeners can follow the line of reasoning and the organization, development, and style are appropriate to task, purpose, and audience.
5. Make strategic use of digital media and visual displays of data to express information and enhance understanding of presentations.
6. Adapt speech to a variety of contexts and communicative tasks, demonstrating command of formal English when indicated or appropriate.

It is hard to argue with the case for these topics presented in the introduction to the Common Core ELA/Literacy standards document (CCSSI, 2010a). Why "comprehension and collaboration"?

To build a foundation for college and career readiness, students must have ample opportunities to take part in a variety of rich, structured conversations—as part of a whole class, in small groups, and with a partner. Being productive members of these conversations requires that students contribute accurate, relevant information; respond to and develop what others have said; make comparisons and contrasts; and analyze and synthesize a multitude of ideas in various domains. (p. 22)

## Why "presentation of knowledge and ideas"?

New technologies have broadened and expanded the role that speaking and listening play in acquiring and sharing knowledge and have tightened their link to other forms of communication. The Internet has accelerated the speed at which connections between speaking, listening, reading, and writing can be made, requiring that students be ready to use these modalities nearly simultaneously. (p. 48)

These statements are obviously true. What is less obvious is that students don't develop these skills without direct instruction. To guide that instruction, each anchor standard has a grade-level version (one each in grades K–8, then one for grades 9–10 and one for grades 11–12). The grade-level versions become increasingly complex as students get older, and when we look at all the grade-level versions of a standard together, we can trace, step by step, how students are expected to progress. The foundational skills they acquire in the early grades will be applied and expanded in later grades until they reach the proficiency level described in the anchor standard. We'll look at the progressions of all the Common Core's speaking and listening standards in the chapters to come. Flip ahead for a preview, or go to corestandards.org.

The Common Core requires teachers to redefine the words "listening" and "speaking" and to embrace rigor. It's no longer enough to rely on students' reassurance that, yes, they heard what we said in the lecture, what their classmate said in a discussion, or what the expert in the online video said; now we must teach students to *evaluate* what they heard and how it was presented. Similarly, nearly all teachers have students give presentations and have done so forever, but now we are called on to spend time teaching students to effectively use digital media to enhance those presentations. We're expected to teach students how to adapt their speech for various contexts and tasks. In short, the Common Core standards push us to do more than we have become accustomed to doing to promote listening and speaking skills. This is a good thing.

## Scaffolding for Strong Instruction

The clear expectations that the Common Core standards offer from grade to grade are a feature that is not discussed often enough. Think about your school. Teachers at each grade level operate independently, for the most part. Few 7th grade teachers stand in front of the class and say, "I know that last year, you focused a lot on main ideas, and you were taught to notice whether or not those ideas were supported by evidence. This year, we will go a bit further, and you will learn to evaluate the soundness of the evidence for claims." Although 11th grade teachers can be pretty sure their students have some experience doing research, not that many can say with certainty, "Last year, you worked on evaluating credibility of sources. This year, you will continue to do that; in addition, you'll work on examining discrepancies among sources."

In my teaching days, when it came to figuring out the content my students had been exposed to, all I had to go on was a very general sense informed by what I knew about my colleagues and what I saw from my students: "Ah, you must have had Mr. Hernandez, because he really stresses the need for a powerful conclusion." "Oh, you know about the federal deficit? Ms. Kinley has a unit about that, and I bet you were in her class." It would have been refreshing to have known that all of my students had had consistent instruction. It would have been beneficial to have known which skills and knowledge I could expect them to have when they arrived in my classroom, as that would have helped me address knowledge and skill gaps more effectively. And it would have been helpful to have had a very clear sense of what my students needed to be prepared to do before they left my classroom so that I could deliberately scaffold those skills over the course of the school year. The structure of the Common Core standards provides that kind of guidance.

Let's be clear, though: I am not suggesting (nor are the Common Core standards suggesting) that we all teach the same content in the same way. Content consistency doesn't mean classroom conformity. For example, Mr. Weiss loved teaching with political cartoons, which he found to be an excellent way to generate interest in topics for discussions. Charged with getting his 7th grade students to understand the Second Amendment and to meet the grade-level expectations for Speaking and Listening Standard 2—"Analyze the main ideas and supporting details presented in diverse media and formats (e.g., visually, qualitatively, orally) and explain how the ideas clarify a topic, text, or issue under study"—he might select a cartoon that made a point about gun control. After discussing the main idea of the cartoon, motivated students would dig deeper into the issues surrounding the Second Amendment, looking for details and evidence that might support or contradict the cartoonist's point of view. Mr. Weiss could then make sure students connected the point of the cartoon to the ideas they found in their research.

Contrast that approach with the approach of Ms. Jefferson, who loved using music to engage her students. Also needing to cover the Second Amendment and the 7th grade version of Standard 2, she might find a song with a message relating to that topic as her hook and instructional medium. For example, a seemingly lighthearted song that contained the lyrics "All the kids with the pumped-up kicks better run better run [sic], faster than my bullets" might be the springboard to get her 7th graders thinking about guns and the pervasiveness of guns in American culture. "What does it say about our culture," I can imagine Ms. Jefferson saying, "that school shootings are written about in popular songs? Is this the result of the Second Amendment?" Her students would then search for information to inform a knowledgeable discussion of the topic, on their way to the same destination Mr. Weiss set for his class: connecting main ideas across various media.

The same standard can also be addressed in other curricular areas. Mr. Goto, a science teacher with no interest in cartoons or music, might show his students a video about stem cell research. Then, during the subsequent discussion, he would check for an understanding of the main ideas and supporting details and challenge students to explain how the video added to the understanding they had from the textbook reading.

What I want to convey here is that that despite the diversity of approaches individual teachers might take, with a clearly articulated content progression, as the teacher in the next grade level, I could be confident that students would come to my 8th grade class knowing how to look for and compare main ideas and supporting details, no matter how they were presented. I could focus on extending those skills to include understanding the motives behind the idea's presentation, a skill required by the 8th grade version of Standard 2.

The Common Core standards tell us where we are going, then, but they don't tell us how to get there. How to get there is what the rest of this book is about. We'll look at each of the six standards in the Speaking and Listening strand and examine the grade-level specifics. I'll suggest ways you can teach the skills needed to master the standards. But let me say it once more: these skills are not just Common Core skills. Although I want to address concerns surrounding Common Core implementation, it's more important to me (and, I'm sure, to you, too) to focus on how to prepare students for life-long success.

# 3

# COLLABORATING/DISCUSSING

Teachers ask students to work in groups all the time. Because working with others is a tricky business, most teachers also spend a fair amount of time putting out the fires caused by friction within groups. Collaboration is difficult. It requires individuals to agree on a goal, divide a task into pieces, delegate the responsibilities, and agree on how to combine all the pieces to accomplish the desired end result.

A key element of collaboration is that it brings people together to *achieve something that could not be achieved individually.* An obvious example would be the U.S. national space program. No one person could design the communication system and the propulsion system, build the fuel tanks and the computer screen, design the logo for the patches, lobby Congress for funding, and so on. For astronauts to go to space and return, a lot of people with unique talents must pool their abilities.

At the same time, it's a mistake to see collaboration as something that's only necessary on giant, unique efforts like the space program. We live in an age of increasing complexity and specialization, and fewer and fewer kinds of work can be done by an individual working alone. This book, for example, is a collaborative effort. I was assisted by an editor, a copyeditor, a graphic designer, a typesetter, and a printing company; without all of us working together, you would not be reading these words now. Amazingly to me, all of this collaboration occurred across the country and without face-to-face interaction. As Grace Rubenstein (2008) has said, "Information age, rest in pieces. This is the Collaboration Age. We can all connect instantly across time zones and oceans. Previously impossible partnerships now produce startling innovations" (¶1–2).

Rubenstein goes on to note that this model of collaboration is open to students, too. Increasingly, they are collaborating beyond the classroom walls—with outside experts (as I did, when I "Skyped in" to help a class of Illinois 8th graders prepare for a presentation) and with fellow students on the other side of the district or the other side of the world. The Global Education Conference (www. globaleducationconference.com) is a great example of classroom-to-classroom interaction and collaboration that operates across national boundaries and oceans.

What's critical to remember is that these collaborative activities, whether conducted within the classroom or at extreme long distance, are almost entirely dependent on listening and speaking. Unless students know how to listen effectively, they cannot fully understand the ideas of their collaborators; without effective speaking skills, they cannot communicate the ideas they are trying to contribute to the collaborative effort.

## A Look at Standard 1

The first of the Common Core's standards for Speaking and Listening (SL.1) is focused squarely on collaborative discussion. Its goal? To graduate students able to **"prepare for and participate effectively in a range of conversations and collaborations with diverse partners, building on others' ideas and expressing their own clearly and persuasively."** In terms of total words, Standard 1 is by far the longest standard within the Speaking and Listening strand, and it's the only one with detailed subcomponents. Here are the grade-level expectations for Standard 1. Note that the italic text indicates aspects of the standard that are new—introduced at the specified grade level rather than continued from the year before, meaning they are important targets for teachers at that grade level. Remember, the Common Core standards are designed to be progressive and to build toward each anchor standard.

**Kindergarten:** Participate in collaborative conversations with diverse partners about kindergarten topics and texts with peers and adults in small and larger groups.

a. Follow agreed-upon rules for discussions (e.g., listening to others and taking turns speaking about the topics and texts under discussion).

b. Continue a conversation through multiple exchanges.

**Grade 1:** Participate in collaborative conversations with diverse partners about grade 1 topics and texts with peers and adults in small and larger groups.

a. Follow agreed-upon rules for discussions (e.g., listening to others *with care, speaking one at a time* about the topics and texts under discussion).

b. *Build on others' talk in conversations by responding to the comments of others* through multiple exchanges.

c. *Ask questions to clear up any confusion about the topics and texts under discussion.*

**Grade 2:** Participate in collaborative conversations with diverse partners about grade 2 topics and texts with peers and adults in small and larger groups.

a. Follow agreed-upon rules for discussions (e.g., *gaining the floor in respectful ways,* listening to others with care, speaking one at a time about the topics and texts under discussion).

b. Build on others' talk in conversations *by linking their comments to the remarks of others.*

c. Ask *for clarification and further explanation as needed* about the topics and texts under discussion.

The primary grades' focus is on the social skills of listening—listen to others, one at a time, raise your hand, and so on. The deeper listening skills are indicated by the grades 1 and 2 expectation that students ask questions to clear up confusion. That can only be done if students interact with what they hear, realizing that their understanding is incomplete. Teachers prompt students: "Do you have any questions?" "Do you all understand how to play Pooh sticks?"

**Grade 3:** *Engage effectively in a range* of collaborative discussions *(one-on-one, in groups, and teacher-led)* with diverse partners on grade 3 topics and texts, *building on others' ideas and expressing their own clearly.*

a. *Come to discussions prepared, having read or studied required material; explicitly draw on that preparation and other information known about the topic to explore ideas under discussion.*

b. Follow agreed-upon rules for discussions (e.g., gaining the floor in respectful ways, listening to others with care, speaking one at a time about the topics and texts under discussion).

c. Ask questions *to check understanding of information presented, stay on topic,* and link their comments to the remarks of others.

d. *Explain their own ideas and understanding in light of the discussion.*

**Grade 4:** Engage effectively in a range of collaborative discussions (one-on-one, in groups, and teacher-led) with diverse partners on grade 4 topics and texts, building on others' ideas and expressing their own clearly.

a. Come to discussions prepared, having read or studied required material; explicitly draw on that preparation and other information known about the topic to explore ideas under discussion.

b. Follow agreed-upon rules for discussions and *carry out assigned roles.*

c. *Pose and respond to specific* questions to clarify or follow up on information*, and make comments that contribute to the discussion* and link to the remarks of others.

d. *Review the key ideas expressed* and explain their own ideas and understanding in light of the discussion.

**Grade 5:** Engage effectively in a range of collaborative discussions (one-on-one, in groups, and teacher-led) with diverse partners on grade 5 topics and texts, building on others' ideas and expressing their own clearly.

a. Come to discussions prepared, having read or studied required material; explicitly draw on that preparation and other information known about the topic to explore ideas under discussion.

b. Follow agreed-upon rules for discussions and carry out assigned roles.

c. Pose and respond to specific questions by making comments that contribute to the discussion and *elaborate o*n the remarks of others.

d. Review the key ideas expressed and *draw conclusions* in light of *information and knowledge gained from* the discussions.

In upper elementary, two significant expectations are added. First, the standards add a preparation piece. Students are expected to read and study before coming to the discussion and to use the material they studied in their comments. We move discussions away from opinion spouting. Second, students are expected to explain the key ideas and how those ideas have influenced their thinking. Teachers have to ask, "In light of what you just heard, how have your own thoughts changed?"

**Grade 6:** Engage effectively in a range of collaborative discussions (one-on-one, in groups, and teacher-led) with diverse partners on grade 6 topics, texts, *and issues,* building on others' ideas and expressing their own clearly.

a. Come to discussions prepared, having read or studied required material; explicitly draw on that preparation *by referring to evidence on the topic, text, or issue to probe and reflect on ideas under discussion.*

b. Follow rules for *collegial* discussions, *set specific goals and deadlines, and define individual roles as needed.*

c. Pose and respond to specific questions *with elaboration and detail* by making comments that contribute *to the topic, text, or issue* under discussion.

d. Review the key ideas expressed and *demonstrate understanding of multiple perspectives through reflection and paraphrasing.*

**Grade 7:** Engage effectively in a range of collaborative discussions (one-on-one, in groups, and teacher-led) with diverse partners on grade 7 topics, texts, and issues, building on others' ideas and expressing their own clearly.

a. Come to discussions prepared, having read *or researched* material under study; explicitly draw on that preparation by referring to evidence on the topic, text, or issue to probe and reflect on ideas under discussion.

b. Follow rules for collegial discussions, *track progress toward* specific goals and deadlines, and define individual roles as needed.

c. Pose questions *that elicit elaboration and respond to others' questions and comments with relevant observations and ideas that bring the discussion back on topic as needed.*

d. *Acknowledge new information expressed by others and, when warranted, modify their own views.*

**Grade 8:** Engage effectively in a range of collaborative discussions (one-on-one, in groups, and teacher-led) with diverse partners on grade 8 topics, texts, and issues, building on others' ideas and expressing their own clearly.

a. Come to discussions prepared, having read or researched material under study; explicitly draw on that preparation by referring to evidence on the topic, text, or issue to probe and reflect on ideas under discussion.

b. Follow rules for collegial discussions *and decision making*, track progress toward specific goals and deadlines, and define individual roles as needed.

c. Pose questions *that connect the ideas of several speakers* and elicit elaboration, and respond to others' questions and comments with relevant evidence, observations, and ideas.

d. Acknowledge new information expressed by others, and, when warranted, *qualify or justify their own views and understanding in light of the evidence presented.*

Middle school students are expected to have mastered the same skills that the preceding grades developed: follow rules, come prepared, refer to material, ask questions, and so on. The subtle shift in the middle school standards is the emphasis on more direct interactions with others. Elicit elaboration from others, connect the ideas of several others, demonstrate understanding of multiple perspectives, respond to others' questions, acknowledge information presented by others—all of these increase the collaborative nature of discussions. Teacher comments should promote these ends: "How can we tie all of this together?" "What else should we ask Martin to help us understand his point?" It's also significant that, for the first time, the standard suggests that listeners need to bring some open-mindedness to the discussion and, "when warranted," modify their views. The teacher might ask, "Whose opinion has shifted? How? Why?"

**Grades 9–10:** *Initiate and participate* effectively in a range of collaborative discussions (one-on-one, in groups, and teacher-led) with diverse partners on grades 9–10 topics, texts, and issues, building on others' ideas and expressing their own clearly *and persuasively.*

a. Come to discussions prepared, having read *and researched* material under study; explicitly draw on that preparation by referring to evidence from texts and other research on the topic or issue to *stimulate a thoughtful, well-reasoned exchange of ideas.*

b. *Work with peers to set rules for collegial discussions and decision making (e.g., informal consensus, taking votes on key issues, presentation of alternate views),* clear goals and deadlines, and individual roles as needed.

c. *Propel conversations* by posing and responding to questions that relate the current discussion *to broader themes or larger ideas; actively incorporate others into the discussion; and clarify, verify, or challenge ideas and conclusions.*

d. *Respond thoughtfully to diverse perspectives, summarize points of agreement and disagreement, and,* when warranted, qualify or justify their own views *and understanding and make new connections* in light of the evidence *and reasoning* presented.

**Grades 11–12:** Initiate and participate effectively in a range of collaborative discussions (one-on-one, in groups, and teacher-led) with diverse partners on grades 11–12 topics, texts, and issues, building on others' ideas and expressing their own clearly and persuasively.

a. Come to discussions prepared, having read and researched material under study; explicitly draw on that preparation by referring to evidence from texts and other research on the topic or issue to stimulate a thoughtful, well-reasoned exchange of ideas.

b. Work with peers to *promote civil, democratic* discussions and decision making, set clear goals and deadlines, and *establish* individual roles as needed.

c. Propel conversations by posing and responding to questions that *probe reasoning and evidence; ensure a hearing for a full range of positions on a topic or issue;* clarify, verify, or challenge ideas and conclusions; *and promote divergent and creative perspectives.*

d. Respond thoughtfully to diverse perspectives; *synthesize comments, claims, and evidence made on all sides of an issue; resolve contradictions when possible; and determine what additional information or research is required to deepen the investigation or complete the task.*

High school students are asked to take more responsibility for discussion. They don't engage in (presumably teacher-created) discussions; they *initiate* discussions, *set* the goals, *establish* the roles. They don't *follow* rules; they *set* the rules. They don't merely listen to others; they actively bring others into the discussion and promote differing perspectives. Teachers are guides, not leaders, and should ask questions instead of giving directives: "What rules should we have for the discussion?" "How can we be sure that we have heard all views?" High school students are charged with resolving contradictions. Teachers should ask, "How can this be solved? Is there new evidence or a new argument that we need?"

For the most part, Standard 1 is pretty straightforward. There is one thing that I would like to highlight, however. This standard asks students to "participate in collaborative conversations" and "engage effectively in a range of collaborative discussions." It is the insertion of the word *collaborative* that merits our particular attention.

## What Makes a Discussion Collaborative?

Does this exchange seem familiar?

> *Teacher:* What did you think of what the author said?
>
> *Student A:* I agree with him. I think that music and art are, like, important to school, and we shouldn't, like, cut them to have more time for math and stuff.
>
> *Student B:* Yeah. I really like art, and I'm good at it. Why should I learn algebra if I will never use it, ya know?
>
> *Student C:* But music class is dumb! I hate singing, and no one plays violin anymore—music is created on a computer now. School should, like, teach computer stuff and video games and things kids do. I mean, not like teach how to *play* a game, but teach how to make games, know what I mean?

Although topics change and speakers build on the previous comments, this "discussion" is really just a collection of students' personal opinions. It's not that there's no value in this kind of activity. Arguably, it gives students practice forming and articulating ideas, which is a core component of effective speaking, and perhaps they gain insight into how others can have diverse and differing opinions. But think how much deeper the inquiry might go and how much more could be gained through more significant interaction that involves deliberate listening as well as speaking. When we require that a discussion be *collaborative*, we set a new slate of expectations.

In the sense that collaboration is doing something within a group, "collaborative discussion" might strike some as a big "duh." How could you have a discussion all by yourself? A better, more precise definition of collaboration would be that it's not just doing something within a group but, rather, interacting with others in that group order to accomplish a goal. Yes, we all have opinions, but why are we getting together to share them? Where is this going? For a discussion to have solid learning value, it must also have a point.

You may be familiar with a story told by Robert Stephens, who founded the Geek Squad team of tech specialists at the Best Buy electronics store chain. Stephens's idea was to have the tech staff at different stores communicate with one another to share problem-solving knowledge. If a customer were to come into a store in Aurora with a problem the Aurora Geek Squad hadn't seen before, they could work with Geek Squad members at the Portland and Gainesville stores who might have solution. With a goal of getting all Geek Squad members prepared to handle whatever problems came to the service desk, Stephens created a wiki, thinking that staff could use it to collaborate and share ideas. What these Geeks did instead was choose their own unique platform for collaborative discussion: an online game called Battlefield 2 where players converse with each other as they run around fighting. Two points stand out here: first, collaborative discussions occur when discussion members are working toward a genuine and specific purpose; second, when group members are given freedom to use the tools they are comfortable with, discussions will blossom in surprising ways.

Now, to a key point we often miss: if something can be done just as well by an individual, collaboration is not necessary. Putting students in a group and asking the group to write a report on the endangered tree octopus of Oregon is not a good way to model collaboration. These are the situations likely to generate the kind of friction that makes group work difficult to manage. The reason we get complaints like, "Teacher, Amanda is doing all the work and won't let us do anything!" is generally because Amanda *can* do all the work by herself. The challenge is to design collaborative activities that actually *require* collaboration. We can look to the principles behind collaborative activities and projects to help us create strong collaborative conversations.

Consider peer editing, for example. Tami and Dave are working on a short story as a peer editing pair. Tami believes what she has written is perfectly clear. Only by discussing it with Dave and listening to his questions will she find out that her story is missing important details. In Dave's story, he wrote, "The teacher gave the tablet to her and I" because somewhere in his educational career, he was taught that the other person comes first and "_____ and I" is always, *always* correct. It takes Tami pointing out the difference between subjective and objective case for Dave to agree to make the change to "her and me." What these examples model is the way a discussion can be used to achieve an end that an individual alone could not achieve. "Two heads are better than one" only if two (or more) heads point us to new understandings and results.

Peer editing, by nature, is set up to promote collaboration. It can be challenging to structure other kinds of classroom conversations this way, but it's necessary. Let's look now at how to do it.

## ⊃ TAKE ACTION: Developing Collaborative Discussion Skills

The strategies in this section are designed to move students from discussion to *collaborative* discussion. They encourage students to talk *with* others rather than *at* others to achieve a meaningful end. These are not directives ("Always assign roles!") but rather *directions* that will help you guide students to more meaningful interactions. Next to each activity title is an indication of the grade levels for which that activity might be most useful. This is not a directive, either. You know your students, and if an activity seems appropriate for them, please use it.

### Structure the physical environment (6–12)

Leslie was my supervising teacher when I was a student teacher. On the first day of school in August, students walked into her 6th grade classroom and found all the desks in the middle of the room and all the chairs around the outside of the room. They stood around bewildered. In their experience, teachers always had the room set up, attractive nameplates were on each desk, and students found their places. This was quite different. Then Leslie began to speak:

> Welcome! I am so happy to see all of you and I hope you had a wonderful summer. I am expecting a great year. But I see that you were expecting a different room arrangement. Let me explain. This year, we will have to work together a lot because often in school and in life, more can be accomplished working with others than can be accomplished working alone. So I figured, why not start now?

You need to work together to arrange the furniture. What will the best setup be? How can the desks be arranged to help all of us learn? Where should you sit? Do some of you need to be up front in order to hear, see, or focus better? Do some of you know you should not sit together because you will be too tempted to pay attention to each other rather than your work? Justine has an aide with her. How can she be accommodated? I trust you to make the environment work for every one of us. Ready? *Go!*

The students proceeded to have an initially awkward but ultimately very successful collaborative discussion. They built on one another's ideas, incorporating them into a design that met all of the expressed needs. The room took shape... but it was not the shape a less flexible teacher would tolerate. I went on to teach for 21 years, and every year, I opened the school year with this activity.

Even if you are not comfortable starting the year this way, there's still a lot you can do to structure the environment to support collaboration. If you have desks, arrange and rearrange them for optimal listening and speaking. Push two desks together to facilitate Think-Pair-Share activities; push four desks together to facilitate teamwork; move all the desks into a large circle for your whole-class discussions so that everyone can see the faces of their classmates; put the desks in rows when the class is listening to student presentations. If you have tables instead of desks, your options may be more limited, but the room can still be modified to fit the situation. In addition to making it easier for communication, restructuring the environment helps students get into the right mindset for it. The arrangement is a cue to the kind of thinking, listening, and speaking that they are about to do.

### Focus students on the process behind learning tasks (4–12)

Have you ever put students in groups and asked them to check their work? The "discussions" can be quite brief. "I got 7." "Me, too." "So did I." The first three students to respond might all have made the same mistake, of course. A person in the group who has the correct answer might just change it, thinking the majority is probably correct. Instead of collaborating to make sure everyone understood the process involved in getting to the solution, the students merely voted on an answer. How can we avoid this type of situation?

Teachers at the College Preparatory School in Oakland, California, have a unique way of encouraging discussion. As reported on Edutopia, math teachers hand out worksheets to each member of a four-person group. While each worksheet focuses on the same algorithmic process, each student receives a unique problem. They might all get the same formula—say, $8 + a \times b - 14 \div c$—but each student receives different values. For one student, $a = 12$, $b = 5$, and $c = 6$; for another, $a = 6$, $b = 14$, and $c = 5$. They plug the values into the problems and get different answers, leading to a discussion that is not about right/wrong but about the order of operations and making sure everyone in the group understand the process (Edutopia Staff, 2012). In the same vein, you might ask students to solve for $y$, but give one student $4y + 3x = 11$ and give another $5y + 4x = 18$. Here again, they cannot rely on one person to provide "the answer"; they have to discuss the process instead.

In a lesson on comma usage, give each student in a group a different piece of writing to edit. The discussion will be about whether there are any introductory phrases in each paper, or whether there are any items in a series. In a science class, give students different procedures, challenging them to identify the control, constants, and variable and explain the thinking involved. This avoids the quick discussion led by the forceful talker ("The variable is the temperature." "I agree." "OK, let's put that down.") and gets to the learning desired ("In my procedure, the temperature changes every time." "In mine, the temperature stays the same, but the amount of time changes." "So in the first one the temperature is a variable but in the second it is a constant?"). Activities such as these give students opportunities to pose and respond to questions in order to check understanding and gain clarity.

### Require groups to collaborate to produce a single product (4–12)

Picture a small group of students engaged in a peer editing assignment. Suggestions are given to Student A, but he ignores them, believing that he knows more than the others do. Have you ever witnessed something like that? It's all too common when students engage in group work in which they do not *have to* collaborate and do not *have to* reach a collective agreement. We need to restructure these activities in a way that trains students for the open-minded listening that collaboration requires.

Try this activity. Hand out a difficult article to each member of the group and ask members to read it, discuss it, and then produce a single summary—one piece of writing that they all agree captures the article's key points. When I used this technique, I would occasionally require students to submit these papers for a grade and ask them to give me a single handwritten document with Student A writing the first sentence, Student B writing the second sentence, Student C writing the third sentence, and so on. As one student in the group writes, the others watch carefully, offering corrections and suggestions to make sure that the group paper is representative of their understanding. For this activity to succeed, students must listen to each other and must effectively express and sometimes argue for their position ("True, the author says that, but I think his main point is _____ because..." or "That needs to be capitalized because..."). As students negotiate what each sentence will say, they practice valuable communication skills.

A variation on this for test time is to distribute copies of the test and put students in groups to discuss answers. Explain that you will be scoring only one copy of the test, selected at random, from each group; all group members will get that test-taker's grade. If students disagree about an answer, they must collaborate to resolve those differences, and some students will realize the need to modify their own views.

## Allow groups to collaborate and then generate individual products (K–12)

Some students strongly dislike getting a "group grade." I understand that thinking, and I don't want to suggest that there is no collaboration unless there is one product. We can let students share ideas to gain an understanding of a concept that they might not have realized on their own and then let each student independently demonstrate that understanding. It's OK to give students an assignment and let them discuss it with each other and share ideas, but then allow each student to turn in his or her own product.

For example, after showing a video on the effects of alcohol on the body, put students in small groups. Explain that each one will need to write a paragraph containing a powerful topic sentence and three supporting sentences that summarizes the main ideas of the video. Allow time for them to share their ideas and get feedback from other group members before sitting down to write.

### Assign roles in group work (K–8)

Giving students specific jobs underscores the value and purpose of collaboration: to combine our efforts and achieve more together than we could alone. When you do this, list the role each member will take, what the expectations of the role are, and the amount of time they will have to do their part. Here are some of the typical jobs group members take on:

- Writer/recorder (takes notes on group discussions)
- Timekeeper (paces the group to make sure the work will be completed on time)
- Summarizer/paraphraser (restates comments and makes sure everyone understands)
- Messenger (goes to get/drop off materials)
- Questioner (goes to other groups or the teacher to ask questions that come up)
- Keyboarder (inputs into the computer or tablet)
- Noise monitor (self-explanatory!)
- Supervisor (keeps everyone on task)
- Reader (reads aloud the assignment/requirements/prompts)
- Reporter (gives an oral report of the group's work to class or teacher)

You may have noticed that some of these roles emphasize listening and speaking more than others. The writer/recorder must listen well to document the group activity; the summarizer must be adept at paraphrasing; the questioner must listen well to understand the issues the group wants addressed and must communicate the questions effectively to those from whom she seeks help; the reporter should call upon good presentation techniques as he speaks. Make sure to assign students different roles during the year so each student can develop a full range of listening and speaking skills.

A Jigsaw activity is another version of this approach. To illustrate, when I taught solids, liquids, and gases in science, I put students into three groups of 10. Group A got together and studied all the materials I had collected about solids, Group B studied liquids, and Group C studied gases. Each group had to agree on the key facts to be presented about their topic and the method for presenting those facts. When all group members were satisfied with their decisions, I had each group count off from 1 to 10, and then I formed new groups: 1s together, 2s together, 3s together, and so on, so that each group had an A person, a B person, and a C person. Then each student took a turn teaching the others about their original group topic. At the end of the process, every student had learned about solid, liquids, and gases. That end is only achieved if students successfully fulfill their defined individual roles. Of course it helps if students know how to be good listeners. Good listening is easier when strong speaking skills are used.

### Find concrete ways to illustrate and promote participation (K–8)

In every class there are some students who dominate the discussions and some students who never say a word. However, our goal is to develop listening and speaking skill in *all* students. We need to make sure every student not only has the chance to participate but is also encouraged to do so. We can accomplish this by handing out poker chips or something similar. Give each child one chip. Describe the rules:

> In today's discussion, when you make a comment, I will take away your chip and not call on you to contribute again until I have collected chips from all of your classmates. Think carefully. Those of you who have lots of opinions, do you want to jump in quickly and

"spend" your chip right away? Those who like to hang back and say nothing, know that you must spend a chip. You need to think about where you will enter the discussion. Today, no one will dominate and no one will be silent.

Depending on the situation, give each student two chips or three chips, or let each student decide whether to take two chips or just one. This is a simple way to ensure that all students have a chance to make comments and respond thoughtfully.

### Employ technology to encourage and support collaboration (6–12 with Padlet; 9–12 with Voicethread)

There is no stand-alone technology standard in the Common Core State Standards. The assumption is that teachers and students will naturally use the tools at their disposal, integrating as needed to achieve learning goals:

> Students employ technology thoughtfully to enhance their reading, writing, speaking, listening, and language use.... They are familiar with the strengths and weaknesses of various technological tools and mediums and can select and use those best suited to their communication goals. (CCSSI, 2010a, p. 7)

I can recommend two easy-to-use websites*.

VoiceThread (www.voicethread.com) is a paid-subscription website that allows users to set up online discussions. A teacher can set up an account, register students, and post online discussion prompts (an article, a picture, a video, and so forth), and then send students the URL for the discussion. When students log in, they have the UDL-friendly option to comment by typing or by voice recording. I've seen quiet students, students who need time to formulate an idea, tech geeks, and others who rarely comment in class become quite "vocal" in the VoiceThread format (Palmer, 2012).

---

*It is dangerous to recommend a website in a print book, as the Internet changes quickly. There are many sites similar to the ones I suggest, and new sites are created daily, so if these disappear, a web search will discover alternatives that accomplish the same end.

Padlet (www.padlet.com) is a website that allows users to post a digital "sticky note" to a discussion board. It is free to register and easy to create a "wall" where students can post brief comments or attach documents, pictures, links, or videos. I recommend Padlet as a way to extend class discussions and have students collaborate on homework assignments. If a difficult problem comes up in a math assignment, for example, students can go online and post notes asking for or giving help. Students who are reluctant to engage in class discussions can comment virtually. See Figure 3.1 for a picture of a sample Padlet board.

Recalling the Best Buy Geek Squad and their game-based tech discussions, look to your students as resources for other ideas. They may have their own places where they chat. Encourage them to create and share their own blogs, discussion boards, and more with the class (as appropriate).

### CAUTION: Don't overdo it

In the best-selling book *Quiet,* author Susan Cain (2012) notes that anywhere from one-third to one-half of us are introverts. It's a

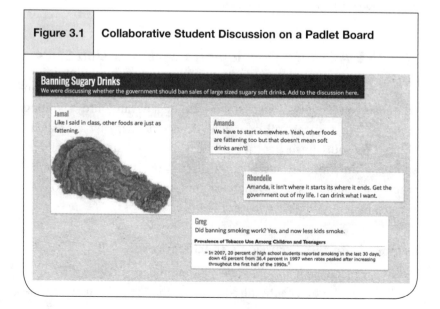

| Figure 3.1 | Collaborative Student Discussion on a Padlet Board |

**Banning Sugary Drinks**
We were discussing whether the government should ban sales of large sized sugary soft drinks. Add to the discussion here.

Jamal
Like I said in class, other foods are just as fattening.

Amanda
We have to start somewhere. Yeah, other foods are fattening too but that doesn't mean soft drinks aren't!

Rhondelle
Amanda, it isn't where it starts its where it ends. Get the government out of my life. I can drink what I want.

Greg
Did banning smoking work? Yes, and now less kids smoke.
Prevalence of Tobacco Use Among Children and Teenagers

» In 2007, 20 percent of high school students reported smoking in the last 30 days, down 45 percent from 36.4 percent in 1997 when rates peaked after increasing throughout the first half of the 1990s.⁹

surprisingly high percentage—probably because so many introverts learn at a very young age how to act like extroverts. The takeaway for teachers is that we probably have more introverts in our classes than we think we do. The movement, stimulation, and collaborative work that extroverts thrive on can be draining on introverts, who tend to prefer lectures and working independently.

As an introvert myself, I understand the discomfort of fitting in with the dominant style of our schools, which are definitely designed for extroverts. Many teachers assume that an active, somewhat noisy, organized-into-groups classroom is proof of great engagement and learning, and we tend to encourage the quieter and more reserved children in our classes to become more vocal and gregarious. This can be inappropriate.

Yes, *all* children need to develop listening and speaking skills, so we cannot excuse students who prefer to work independently from all group activities or all presentations. That is why I mentioned the poker chip discussion as a way to push the quiet students to gain needed oral communication skill and why I suggested online tools that are introvert-friendly. But we can remember that it is necessary to vary the structure of our classes to allow for the unique needs of the introverted students just as we allow for the unique needs of other diverse learners.

## ⟳ TAKE ACTION: Developing Civil Discussion Skills

Collaboration cannot occur in a hostile environment. Without an emphasis on civility, discussions can degenerate into shouting matches. We see this all over television: one panelist increasing volume to shut down another panelist as they "discuss" politics, sports, or movies. The essence of discussion is not to make sure your idea dominates but to increase understanding or come to consensus. Incivility does not foster those ends.

### Communicate the discussion's specific focus (K–12)

Every discussion should have an announced and specific focus. Clarifying at the outset the direction that the discussion should be headed is the first step in keeping that discussion on track and on topic. Consider these two prompts and the comments they generate:

*Teacher:* Let's discuss Chapter 7.

*Seth:* Chapter 7? It was too long. I got bored.

*Dani:* Bored? You're crazy. It was awesome.

*Seth:* Awesomely long and boring, you mean. Maybe you have time to read all that, but I got better things to do.

With too little structure, comments degenerate quickly. See here how a clearer focus supports more substantive responses:

*Teacher:* Lots to talk about in Chapter 7. Let's start with this. What do you think Ignatius's motivation could be for taking that job?

*Seth:* I think he wanted to prove he could do something on his own. He had been too influenced by his mother before.

*Dani:* Maybe, but this wasn't his first job. He was on his own before. Maybe there was no motive. Sometimes we just do things without thinking.

Similarly, the very open-ended "Let's discuss obesity" can too easily lead to off-topic musings like

*Sarah:* I knew this really fat kid in my old school....

*Jess:* Does anyone watch that show about fat people trying to lose weight?

A specific prompt ("What are the main causes of obesity?") is likely to elicit more relevant responses:

*Sarah:* Well, that first article we read said high fructose corn syrup can really mess up your metabolism, and it is in lots of soft drinks.

*Jess:* Think about how big a large soft drink at McDonald's is! And fast food in general. People eat a lot of fast food because it's cheap and nobody has time to cook.

When students are focused on the discussion's purpose, they are more likely to concentrate on ideas rather than personalities. State upfront what you intend students to get out of the conversation they're about to take part in (e.g., understand the text better, come to agreement on an action, understand other views on an issue, settle a dispute) so that they know it's not just a platform for forceful students to pontificate. Announcing the focus in advance helps students prepare, too. "We are going to discuss how the Mayan culture was affected by European explorers" gives students a purpose for reading and rereading a required text that a more general statement does not.

### Set rules for civil discussion (K–12)

To students (and to most adults) *discussion* means they get to say what they think. While that may be true, there needs to be a less selfish and more learning-oriented motive. We make that clear when we set specific rules. These rules can also keep us on track when it becomes obvious that our "diverse partners" (per Standard 1) have diverse and sometimes contentious viewpoints. Here are some rules for civil discussion that I recommend, along with a bit of elaboration. Bear in mind that you'll want to adjust the specifics to suit your grade level.

- *Focus on the task at hand.* It's important to convey that discussion means clearing one's desk of unrelated material, removing the distractions of papers, pencils, and other items that may affect the ability to focus.
- *Don't interrupt.* Stress to students that cutting others off is denying them their rightful role in shaping the discussion. It's essential that every speaker be allowed to finish his or her thought.
- *Build on what others say.* Building on the comments of others shows that students are paying attention to one another. Incorporating their comments into a response is a way of showing respect for others' thinking. ("I want to add to what Maruja said...")
- *Control emotions.* If you are selecting good, engaging topics for discussion, at some point the discussion may become heated. It is

important to remind students that outbursts do not advance ideas. Becoming too emotional tends to shut down discussion: the overly emotional listener may be too worked up to effectively understand others; the overly emotional speaker may turn others off if she seems to be berating rather than responding.

• *Control nonverbal signals.* When I was a student, I angered people who disagreed with me… not because of what I said, but because of all the nonverbal messages I sent while they were speaking. Rolling eyes, dismissive shrugs, smirks, flippant hand gestures, and more—even if they're unconscious—convey disrespect and shut down conversation. They are to be avoided.

• *Don't jump to conclusions.* I once made a statement at a conference that the Common Core State Standards are a plot by liberals to expand the role of the national government. Immediately, someone in the audience interrupted me to defend the Common Core. She interrupted just before I could say that the Common Core State Standards are a plot by conservatives to destroy education by setting standards so high that public schools will fail and privatization efforts will win. I was making the point that people have radically different ideas about the standards, and rather than listen to others' opinions, we ought to read the standards and make our own decision about their worth. Assuming that you know where the speaker is going is a mistake to avoid.

• *Don't judge the messenger.* All of us sometimes have to work at separating actors from actions. As I've told my students, I hate cleaning up the mess when my son spills his milk, but I never hate my son for spilling the milk. Stress that expressing an offensive idea doesn't mean the person who expressed that idea is therefore also offensive. Good people can have radically different opinions.

• *Practice empathy.* Some topics have an emotional impact. A health class discussion about the dangers of smoking may affect a child whose parents smoke or whose grandmother died from lung cancer differently than it affects a child whose parents do not smoke. Students need to be sensitive to emotional responses as well as to intellectual responses to truly understand some comments.

- *Be patient.* Note to students that outbursts like "Oooh! Oh! Me next!" suggest that the person making them has decided on a comment to make and is no longer listening to the speaker. Hands should stay down until a speaker is finished.
- *Ask questions.* Students can avoid jumping to conclusions, develop empathy, and encourage elaboration by asking questions before commenting. Initiate and reinforce the habit of asking at least one question of the previous speaker. For example: "You said _____, but would you also say that if the situation were _____?" "You seem upset. Why does it bother you to hear that _____?"
- *Presume positive intentions.* Everyone should enter the discussion with the idea that everyone else participating wants to contribute to a good result.
- *Everyone's contributions are essential.* Sometimes, class leaders can effectively shut down a discussion either by refusing to engage or by offering an opinion or answer that other students are reluctant to challenge. I remember a time in elementary school when I was asked to answer a math problem. I gave the wrong answer, but because I had a reputation as a math geek, once I had answered, the other kids—who might have had the correct answer—put their hands down and refused to share. Convincing students that what they have to say matters is a way to prevent this kind of roadblock, build confidence, and promote sincere expression.

Post, test-drive, and discuss the rules you set. After a few rounds of discussion, prompt students to generate additional rules they all agree to follow.

### Have evidence-based discussions (6–12)

As noted, classroom discussions can very easily devolve into fairly random statements of students' personal opinions. To avoid this and to build students' ability to identify evidence and, ultimately, evaluate the sufficiency of evidence, hold some discussions in which everyone is required to cite a specific piece of evidence to support every comment they make. For example:

*Jake:* Elijah is spineless. I don't respect him because in Chapter 5, when the stranger came into camp, he hid behind the tree.

*Tariq:* I disagree. I think Elijah is smart. Remember that in Chapter 2 someone came into camp and conned them all out of a lot of money. I think Elijah learned to distrust strangers.

*Kayla:* College should *not* be a goal for everyone. My evidence is that the article said that only 30 percent of Americans earn a bachelor's degree. Why force all of us to take college prep classes when more than two-thirds of us won't ever get a degree?

*Tyler:* Just because people don't finish college doesn't mean college prep classes are a bad idea. The video mentioned that people with college degrees make $750,000 more over a lifetime than people without college degrees.

## Use the "traveling debate" approach to build persuasion skills (6–12)

Persuasion—as opposed to bullying and shouting others down—requires civility. One of my favorite ways to encourage civil discussion and build students' persuasive power is the traveling debate, a technique introduced in *Well Spoken* (Palmer, 2011). Begin by selecting a topic about which there are two strongly divided opinions and set up a "yes/no" proposition. For example: should a school official be allowed to punish a student for something that the student posted to a social media site outside of school hours? Have students who say "yes" stand on one side of the room and students who say "no" stand on the other. (There is no middle ground in this exercise; here, the principal either can or cannot punish.) Select one speaker from the Yes side to speak. That speaker's objective is to persuade students on the No side to change their minds. When he has finished speaking, those who have been persuaded silently walk to the Yes side of the room. No applause or comments are allowed. Next, select one speaker from the No side to attempt to persuade

Yes students to change their minds. Continue choosing speakers until everyone has had a turn or until the issue seems exhausted. Traveling debates give students a clear picture of multiple perspectives and a chance, by physically moving, to acknowledge information expressed by others.

Too often, the "discussions" of controversial issues we see in the media are nothing more than an exchange of insults. The crux of this activity is that it challenges students to talk about the issues rather than about the people who hold opposing ideas about those issues. In a traveling debate, no student will be persuaded to change sides if the speaker's argument is "That's just stupid" or "Only an idiot would think that."

## Model civil discussions with online sources (6–12)

Speaking of incivility, the Internet—particularly so-called discussion boards and comments sections—provides plenty of models. We want to replace negative models of discussion with positive ones. ProCon.org (www.procon.org) is a website with the mission of "promoting critical thinking, education, and informed citizenship by presenting controversial issues in a straightforward, nonpartisan, primarily pro-con format" (¶4). Topics are organized for easy searching: Education, Politics, Media & Entertainment, Science & Technology, and so on. Whether students are interested in video games and violence, standardized testing in school, or vegetarianism, they are likely to find an interesting debate on ProCon.org that models civil discourse and the correct use of evidence.

We want students to have meaningful discussions in class. We want students to be able to work together well. We want students to listen and respond well. Recall the quote early in this chapter: "This is the Collaboration Age." We need to work to ensure that students are well prepared for living in this age. That's why many of us will need to increase our efforts to foster the collaboration skills addressed in Standard 1. Adopting some of the strategies suggested in this chapter can help you prepare your students for core assessments *and* later success.

One standard and skill set covered. Our work has just begun.

# 4

# LISTENING/MEDIA LITERACY

Early in my teaching career, I confused good listening with being polite. In retrospect, I taught manners more than I did listening. If my students were sitting quietly and weren't being disruptive, I felt like a success. *They're listening!* I thought. What did I require beyond that? Nothing. What did I teach them about active listening? Nothing. And I was not alone. As Anna Bass (2005) puts it, "Listening is the most used but least taught communication skill" (¶1).

It's no surprise that many of our students (and many adults) struggle as listeners. The problem becomes more severe when we realize that listening now includes more than understanding words that are delivered in person. Today, students listen to diverse media with differing presentation formats. To understand, they must also understand the use of sound, the credibility of Internet sources, the techniques used in video, and more. Let me give an example.

A student is doing research. He finds an article about his topic. In the text is a hyperlink to a video. His reading research just turned into listening research. A dramatic soundtrack and powerful images give the spoken words a lot of impact, and the student is impressed, believing that what he heard is the incontrovertible truth. He fails to understand how the music was used to manipulate his emotions; he fails to recognize that the images selected may not be representative of the whole picture; and he fails to question the reliability of the site in the hyperlink. In other words, he was unprepared for his listening task.

The example makes clear that we have to expand our definition of listening to include media literacy. To meet this expanded definition of listening requires skills that students will not master without direct instruction. That's where we come in.

## A Look at Standard 2

Speaking and Listening Standard 2 (SL.2) provides the Common Core's most concentrated focus on effective listening, which it links to the 21st century skill of media literacy. Although it's a *listening* standard, it is worth pointing out that Standard 2 falls under the heading "Comprehension." The aim, articulated in the anchor standard, is to ensure students graduate high school able to **"integrate and evaluate information presented in diverse media and formats, including visually, quantitatively, and orally."** Let's look at how those skills develop over the course of K–12 instruction.

> **Kindergarten:** Confirm understanding of a text read aloud or information presented orally or through other media by asking and answering questions about key details and requesting clarification if something is not understood.
>
> **Grade 1:** Ask and answer questions about key details *in a text read aloud or information presented orally or through other media.*
>
> **Grade 2:** *Recount or describe key ideas* or details from a text read aloud or information presented orally or through other media.

Here in the primary grades, the objective is to prepare students to ask and answer questions about information they hear. They need to be able to ask questions to be sure they "get it" and be able to recount key ideas so that we, the teachers, can also be sure they get it. Instructionally, teachers take the lead, prompting students to remember and communicate their understanding. ("Did

Winnie-the-Pooh give a balloon to Eeyore for his birthday? Did something happen to the balloon on the way?")

> **Grade 3:** *Determine the main* ideas and *supporting details* of a text read aloud or information presented in diverse media and formats, including visually, quantitatively, and orally.

> **Grade 4:** *Paraphrase portions of a text* read aloud or information presented in diverse media and formats, including visually, quantitatively, and orally.

> **Grade 5:** *Summarize a written text* read aloud or information presented in diverse media and formats, including visually, quantitatively, and orally.

In upper elementary, the focus becomes teaching students to paraphrase and summarize so that they can begin to take control of their remembering and understanding. ("Retell the story. What did Winnie-the-Pooh do for Eeyore's birthday?")

> **Grade 6:** *Interpret information* presented in diverse media and formats (e.g., visually, quantitatively, orally) *and explain how it contributes to a topic, text, or issue under study.*

> **Grade 7:** *Analyze the main ideas and supporting details* presented in diverse media and formats (e.g., visually, quantitatively, orally) and explain *how the ideas clarify* a topic, text, or issue under study.

> **Grade 8:** Analyze *the purpose* of information presented in diverse media and formats (e.g., visually, quantitatively, orally) and *evaluate the motives (e.g., social, commercial, political) behind its presentation.*

In middle school, instruction begins to nudge students toward interpretation and analysis. Implicit in the standards is a move from fiction to nonfiction, from story to information. It is not enough for students to absorb information and grasp main ideas; they must be able to use this information and explain how the information helps them understand the larger concept. ("What information did you learn about polar ice caps by reading this article? How does that information help us understand global warming?") Notice that 8th graders are expected to analyze motives and consider why specific information is being disseminated in the first place. ("Why did the author select these facts to present to you? Is the video producer trying to inform? Persuade?")

> **Grades 9–10:** *Integrate multiple sources* of information presented in diverse media or formats (e.g., visually, quantitatively, orally), evaluating the *credibility and accuracy of each source.*

> **Grades 11–12:** Integrate multiple sources of information presented in diverse formats and media (e.g., visually, quantitatively, orally) *in order to make informed decisions and solve problems,* evaluating the credibility and accuracy of each source and *noting any discrepancies among the data.*

By high school, we require students to integrate multiple sources of information and evaluate the worth of the sources. ("Consider the video we watched, the article we read, and the chapter in our textbook. All of them have different perspectives about climate change. Which one seems most credible to you? Why?") Juniors and seniors are expected to do something with the information. ("Some say climate change is man-made, and we can change our behavior; some say it is not man-made—that human behaviors have no impact; still others say "climate change" is a myth. Where does the disagreement come from? Whom should we believe? What should we do?")

Notice how the focus of Standard 2 changes as students progress toward graduation. By the time they reach middle school, the focus has shifted from questioning in order to understand to grasping how information presented in "diverse media and formats" contributes to understanding; what the motives behind a source are; and how credible a source is. The ability to access this information, understand it, and evaluate it falls under the umbrella term media literacy. In this chapter, we'll look at how effective listening supports the understanding and integration necessary for media literacy and examine ways to teach the skills associated with both.

## Understanding Effective Listening

In an interesting TED talk from 2011, business leader and sound consultant Julian Treasure makes the claim that we spend 60 percent of our communication time listening yet retain just 25 percent of what we hear. Some might quibble with the exact accuracy of this figure, but it is clear that we listen more than we speak, read, or write— possibly more than all three of those combined. It is also clear that 25 percent is a disappointing retention percentage, and I assume Treasure was talking about adults. Maybe I am shortchanging our students, but I believe their retention percentage may be less than the adult figure. There were certainly some students who made me wonder at times if they'd retained *anything* from my class.

What does it take to be a great listener, capable of "integrating and evaluating information presented in diverse media and formats, including visually, quantitatively, and orally"? How can those skills be taught? Where can we find resources to build effective listening skills in our students? In search of answers, I went to teacher bookstores in my area. One store had nothing on listening—not one book about the first and the most important way we learn. The other had four books on the topic, each of which contained different genres of passages to be read aloud. Every passage was followed by a graphic organizer which featured clues about what to listen for in order to be able to provide a fill-in-the-blank answer. While this genre-and-clue approach might be a useful beginning, it won't be sufficient to achieve the standards.

I went home and continued my search online. Prominently displayed on the first results page for "listening skills" was a poster offering the following advice:

**Listening Skills**

1. Sit up.
2. Look interested.
3. Lean forward.
4. Listen.
5. Act interested.
6. Nod your head to show that you are tuned in.
7. Track the speaker with your eyes.

Try this advice with a spouse or loved one: lean forward, nod your head, move your eyes, and *act* interested as he or she is talking. I predict trouble.

Are these habits really what we want students to aim for? Listening involves more than faking specific behaviors. Leaning forward, nodding your head, and so forth may be strong nonverbal cues that a listener can use to show engagement with the speaker, but they have nothing to do with the purpose of listening, which is to understand the speaker's message. The poster conveys the *style* of listening but none of its critical substance.

The next question to consider is *what are we listening to?* At one point in history, there was a simple answer: the in-person human voice and the nonverbal messages communicated through tone, facial expression, hand gestures, and demeanor. Now the variety is mind-boggling. We still listen to the human voice, but we listen to it in person, through a speaker, on a screen, amplified, modulated, and synthesized. We listen to it backed with sound effects, music, natural sounds, digitized creations, and more. There is a lot of input to take in, evaluate, and interpret.

## ⭕ TAKE ACTION: Developing Listening Skills

I made the point that our definition of listening has expanded, but that doesn't mean the original definition should be forgotten. The suggestions that follow all pertain to what we might call "traditional" listening, which is a crucial part of every classroom, every day. They focus not on outward behaviors but on ways to encourage understanding and cognitive interaction with incoming messages. The goal is to help students move beyond passively receiving input.

### Ask students to help define "good listening" (K–12)

I am a big proponent of asking students to think about their thinking and encouraging teachers to provide more metacognitive activities for students of all ages. In the case of listening, we always ask students to *do* it, but we often fail to ask them to get involved in the process of understanding listening and become conscious of that process.

Laura works with the Critical Skills Program at Antioch University New England. She suggests to teachers enrolled in the program that they ask their students to self-generate listening rules. This accomplishes two goals: students actively engage in thinking about listening, and students are more likely to follow the rules because they created the rules. The process is simple: set up a "T chart" and invite students to answer two questions: "What does good listening look like?" and "What does good listening sound like?" Laura advocates prompting students to describe these behaviors. For young children, that might entail asking something like, "If our principal, Mrs. Flamming, walked in here and we were 'good listeners' during story time, what would she see? What would she hear?" Specifics are important. If a student prompted to define good listening calls out "Respect!" some elaboration is necessary: "What does *respect* mean? What would it look like if I were being respectful? How do I show respect?"

Once captured, these descriptions should be used to guide classroom discussions. Shared by Anne, a 4th grade teacher, Figure 4.1 shows a student-generated, behavior-focused definition of what good listening looks like. She posted this chart in a prominent place in her classroom so that she can reference it as she observes students' work: "I am seeing good examples *of kind words* in this group" or "I am not seeing a lot of *looking at each other*. Some of you seem to be looking elsewhere."

### Teach students to listen with purpose (K–12)

There is a difference between *listening* and *listening for*. One of my favorite reading lessons demonstrated to students that we read differently depending on our purpose for reading. I would give students a recipe and ask them to read it with different purposes: to find out if it includes ingredients that are available in the kitchen, to assess if it will be difficult to prepare, to evaluate if the recipe is healthy, and so on. Once everyone had finished reading the recipe, I asked questions, and clear patterns emerged. Readers who read

| Figure 4.1 | Student-Generated Guidelines for "Quality Conversations" |
|---|---|

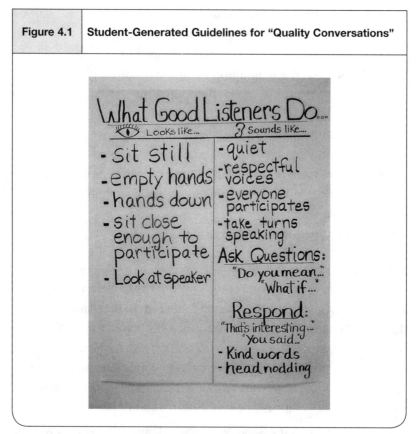

*Source:* Anne Palmer, Cottonwood Creek Elementary, Greenwood Village, Colorado. Used with permission.

with a focus on ingredients did not do well when asked to describe the steps of preparation; readers who focused on technique (how to separate an egg, whip the whites, and fold them into the batter) tended to miss some questions about ingredients.

Introduce students to the idea of listening with purpose by highlighting just how many purposes for listening they might have:

- To remember or understand what happened in a story
- To remember or understand a procedure
- To learn important dates
- To find examples
- To find reasons supporting the main ideas
- To solve a problem

- To find metaphors and similes
- To identify inflections in the speech of the person talking
- To focus on how the speech was delivered
- To focus on the message only, ignoring the delivery
- To identify places where they have questions or need help understanding
- To identify points they agree with
- To identify points they disagree with
- To find errors in verb tense, pronoun use, or word choice
- To find places where they might offer suggestions for improvement in an argument
- To identify how the speaker is feeling

The list could go on and on.

An activity I recommend is to ask students to view a short video several times, giving them something different to listen for each time through. At some point, be sure to turn off the sound so they can "listen" to what the nonverbal cues are saying. A video that works well for the activity is Kid President's "A Pep Talk from Kid President to You" speech, available on YouTube. Try asking students to listen to it with the following purposes:

- To determine the actions Kid President wants us to take
- To identify the different vocal styles he uses to emphasize his points
- To notice how the scene changes/montage affect the message
- To notice how the music in the video contributes to mood

You want students to grasp that listening is not the same thing as passive hearing; it is purposeful, active, and interactive. To listen is to participate as a partner in the speaker's communication.

### Teach about filters (9–12)

Treasure (2011) reminds us that what we hear is affected by our culture, language, values, beliefs, attitude toward the topic or speaker, expectations, and intentions. In other words, all the messages we hear are received through personal filters.

As an example, I recall a faculty meeting called one Friday afternoon so that someone from the district office could introduce us to RTI. At 4:30, after an exhausting week of teaching, the trainer came in with a PowerPoint presentation full of densely packed text. Most of the teachers walked into the meeting feeling at least a little resentful of the scheduling. An hour and a half later, almost everyone walked out with a very negative impression of RTI, not because of anything having to do with RTI itself but because the presentation's timing and design were so poor. Our attitude colored our perception of the message.

Ask students to think about the filters they have. Work with a simple statement such as "Making a lot of money is good." Why might an American hear that phrase differently than a Buddhist monk in Tibet? Would it have something to do with how Americans have been raised with rags-to-riches stories and media models that glorify financial success, while the monk has come to eschew personal possessions? As soon as the American and the Tibetan Buddhist monk hear "Making a lot of money is good," who they are and what they believe instantly and inevitably colors their listening experience. It isn't even necessary to use such a dramatic example. Someone majoring in business will listen with a different bias than someone majoring in social work. Those biases can cause us to tune out parts of the messages we get. Only by being aware of these biases can we become more open and effective listeners.

## Ask students to paraphrase during discussion (4–12)

Attention is a key to effective listening. Too often, students in a discussion group spend too little time listening and too much time waiting to speak. Something a speaker says triggers a thought, the hand goes up, and the ears shut out further input. Even though I ban raising a hand until a speaker has finished, I realize that it's natural for a listener's thoughts to focus less on "What other interesting things are being said?" and more on "Are you done yet so that I can add what I think?" One way to defeat this mindset and get students to really listen is to require them to paraphrase the last comment offered before adding a comment of their own.

*Pepe:* I understood you to say that texting hurts writing skills because when we text, we don't spell well and we don't punctuate. I think that text messages are actually getting rid of stupid ways of spelling. "Enough" is dumb; "e-n-u-f" makes a lot more sense.

*Christina:* Agreed, e-n-o-u-g-h is dumb, and maybe some of the spellings we text do make sense. But "lol" and "btw" and no capital letters and no punctuation slip into formal writing, and that hurts us. Employers will want good memos, good reports, you know?

The goal is not to have students repeat what the previous commenter said but rather to state in their own words the *essence* of what that person said. Listeners must evaluate the message to get to its core and then integrate that information into their comment. This is precisely the focus of Anchor Standard 2. (The specific skill of *paraphrasing,* you might note, is addressed in Standard 2 at the 4th grade level.) You can scaffold this skill's development and encourage its use thereafter by giving students examples of phrases to use:

- So you're suggesting...
- You think that...
- Your plan is to...
- What you are asking is...
- If I am hearing you right, you believe...
- You feel that...
- You disagree with the statement...
- As I understand it, you want to...
- According to you, a good reason to _____ is...
- If you had your way, we would...

## Teach active listening (6–12)

There are many versions of "active listening," but all of them have the same goal: to reframe *how* we listen. As mentioned earlier, hearing is a passive act; it's the receiving of sound. Listening is different; it is a series of constant choices:

- *What to focus on.* The words of the speaker or the street noise outside? The details of the narrative or the thematic elements? The feelings that the speaker is expressing or the feelings that the speaker is evoking?
- *What to respond to.* Say something about this point? Let that point go?
- *How to respond.* Nod head? Make some other sign of agreement or disagreement? Change body language? Formulate a comment of response?
- *When to respond.* Interrupt? Offer ideas when the speaker's finished? After a long pause? After somebody else breaks the ice?

The trick is to move from making these choices automatically, based on habit, to making them purposefully, thoughtfully, and deliberately. You can help your students do that by teaching them the metacognitive skill of monitoring the choices they are making. As far as approaches go, Julian Treasure (2011) suggests taking the Sanskrit word for essence, *rasa,* and using it as an acronym:

> **R**eceive—Pay attention.
> **A**ppreciate—Give small acknowledgements ("Um hum," "Oh yeah," "Sure…").
> **S**ummarize—Repeat the essence ("So you're saying…").
> **A**sk questions—Get clarification or elaboration.

Try sharing this acronym with students, pointing out that RASA is composed of verbs—action words—which emphasize that listening is indeed an active process. If you teach older students, you might challenge them to create their own active listening acronym. Resist, however, the common urge to offer numeric lists: "the 10 keys to active listening" or "the 15 steps of reflective listening." Students, even young ones, are *buried* with lists of things to do and things to think about. Keep it simple.

## Understanding Media Literacy

The original definition of *literacy* relied on the Latin root *littera,* meaning "letters," and referred only to competency in reading and writing. Today *literacy* more commonly means "mastery," and we speak of numerical literacy, computer literacy, and information literacy to name a few. Learning how to understand and effectively use media is part of literacy, too.

When I began my teaching career, school consisted of teachers talking and students reading textbooks and basal readers. Research meant going to the library and pulling volumes of the *World Book Encyclopedia.* Those days are gone. Now, as the language of Standard 2 reminds us, information comes from "diverse media and formats," and students of all ages need to be adept at accessing and evaluating varied forms of input.

Though students are exposed to massive amounts of information inside and outside class, we have not done a very good job of teaching them how to view, listen to, and evaluate that information. For many years, I had "No TV Month" in my class, during which I would ask my students to forgo watching television for a full 30 days. It was a lesson in addiction and self-control, but it was also a lesson in media literacy. Although my students generally spent an average of four hours a day watching television, they didn't think to reflect on television as something that was constructed with goals beyond "be entertaining." They had no idea how the medium operated. They had no answers to questions like, "How many commercials are there per hour?" "What persuasive techniques do those commercials use?" "What is the structure of a sitcom?" and "What stories are on the local news, and why do you think they are chosen?" Now, as students are exposed to more and varied media, becoming media literate is even more important.

Going by the grade-level benchmarks in Standard 2, at age 6, a kindergarten student is expected to *get* information orally and from various media; at age 12, he is expected to *interpret* information presented with diverse media; and at age 15, he is expected to *integrate* information from multiple sources and *evaluate credibility and accuracy* of information presented in diverse media or formats. Remember that all these expectations are grouped under the umbrella of listening. The standard is not asking for students to read information from different sources; it's assuming they will gather and comprehend information from media sources beyond just printed materials.

Some textbook companies are now creating digital textbooks. Students read words on a screen, then watch and listen to embedded videos. I wrote a "Read & Watch" book called *Digitally Speaking: How to Improve Student Presentations with Technology* (2012). This book is only available online; it sits on the cloud waiting to be accessed by any Internet-capable device. It contains videos of teachers and students modeling the suggested activities as well as demonstrations of how to use new digital communication tools. The "reader" is now also a watcher/listener. We need to prepare students for this reality.

Of course much of the input that students receive will not be from a known textbook or educational publisher. How do we help them sift through the barrage of information they are exposed to when we send them out to research? As I work with schools to help them move from being aware of technology to *using* technology, two of my standard questions are, "How many of you have assigned a project where students are told to use the Internet for research?" (almost all hands go up) and "How many of you teach a unit on Internet literacy first?" (almost no hands go up). This is problematic.

*Getting information off the Internet is like taking a drink from a fire hydrant.*

That quote has been attributed to Mitchell Kapor, a computer pioneer and the founder of Lotus. Although he admitted to me that he is unclear about when he said this or whether he actually said it at all, the point is well taken. A Google search of "PVLEGS," an acronym I invented years ago (and that we'll discuss in an upcoming chapter) yielded 453,000 results, even though there is only the one meaning of the word and only one website (mine) that discusses it. A search for a more common topic of interest, "climate change," yielded 578,000,000 results. Imagine a student beginning research and discovering 600 million resources, and Kapor's fire hydrant analogy starts to look understated. The Common Core's Standard 2 for Speaking and Listening correctly foresees that students will need to be able to analyze the purpose, credibility, and accuracy of the inputs available to them.

I recall a day that one of my 6th grade students came running into class shouting, "We are all going to die! They are going to poison our air!" As it turned out, while doing online research for her project on air pollution, she came across a site that called itself the National Center for Atmospheric Study. It had a very impressive and official-seeming seal that looked "governmental." According to the site, enemies of the United States had stockpiled poisonous gases and were going to release them into our air. Our only hope of survival would be to have tanks of oxygen available for all family members for the rest of their lives. I realized then that I should have taught my 6th graders more about the Internet before I sent them off researching, beginning with the warning that they should expect to find claims that are not true.

Today's teacher must help students evaluate the credibility, accuracy, and motives of information presented in diverse media. This includes the Internet, as well as all the other information sources they encounter on a daily basis.

## ⊃ TAKE ACTION: Developing Media Literacy

The previous "Take Action" section in this chapter focused on what I called "traditional" listening. Now I want to cover strategies for helping students become proficient "digital" listeners. Auditory messages are now intertwined with and affected by sound and image. We have to teach students how sounds and images affect listening and give them ways to evaluate that impact.

### Teach visual literacy (4–12)

What we hear is affected by what we see. In the lower grades, it's possible to make this point by simply asking if the image matches the message. For example, "About Me" speeches are a common assignment for young students. A child describing how much she loves soccer undercuts her message if she shows a picture of herself eating birthday cake; she reinforces her message if she shows a picture of herself in uniform and in action at a soccer game. Her audience will have an indelible impression of her soccer mania.

With examples such as these, we can begin to ask students questions about intentions and message construction. What if our soccer player says, "I am a great soccer player" but the picture shows her on the bench watching players on the field? Her audience is likely to think, "She must not be *that* good." What they heard has been altered by the image they see.

In the upper grades, Standard 2 requires students to evaluate how information is delivered. Think of a typical print ad in a magazine. That ad was not constructed in a haphazard way. Camera angle, position of text, the clothing of the people pictured, and the age and type of people pictured were all carefully considered. Visual literacy is the ability to analyze this kind of media and uncover its motives and purposes through systematic examination and questioning. Figure 4.2 shows the Photo Analysis Worksheet created by the education staff at the National Archives and Records Administration (NARA). I recommend all middle and high school teachers adopt or adapt this worksheet and use it to help their students become more active, questioning, and analytic consumers of visual media. It is worth noting that NARA has developed various media analysis tools for audio recording and video as well, and they can be found at www.archives.gov/education/lessons/worksheets/.

### Teach the taxonomy of Internet domain names (6–12)

There is a difference between websites that end in .com, .edu, and .gov, and no teacher should assign any independent Internet research until students can explain what these suffixes suggest about the content the site presents and the motives of the organization providing it. If my 6th grade student who was terrified by the poison gas threat circulated by the National Center for Atmospheric Study had known about domain suffixes, she would have been suspicious when she saw a "governmental" seal on a .com site. Briefly:

- **.com** is the most commonly used extension and the one that comes to mind for most people. The "com" derives from *commercial,* which is *the* signal that there is probably a business focus to the site. Students should expect to see something for sale. A .com domain is

| Figure 4.2 | A Tool for Building Visual Literacy |
|---|---|

Reset Form                    Photo Analysis Worksheet                    Print Form

**Step 1. Observation**

A. Study the photograph for 2 minutes. Form an overall impression of the photograph and then examine individual items. Next, divide the photo into quadrants and study each section to see what new details become visible.

B. Use the chart below to list people, objects, and activities in the photograph.

| People | Objects | Activities |
|---|---|---|
|  |  |  |
|  |  |  |
|  |  |  |
|  |  |  |
|  |  |  |
|  |  |  |
|  |  |  |
|  |  |  |
|  |  |  |

**Step 2. Inference**                    Limit response for each question to 5 lines of text

Based on what you have observed above, list three things you might infer from this photograph.

**Step 3. Questions**

A. What questions does this photograph raise in your mind?

B. Where could you find answers to them?

Reset Form                    **Designed and developed by the**
                    **Education Staff, National Archives and Records Administration,**
                    **Washington, DC 20408**                    Print Form

*Source:* The Education Staff, National Archives and Records Administration. Available: http://www.archives.gov/education/lessons/worksheets/photo_analysis_worksheet.pdf

a "proceed with caution" flag; the information they find may be reliable, but they should watch out for the pitch.

- **.net** is an abbreviation for network. It was originally for businesses that provided the services the web depends upon—Internet service providers and web hosting companies. Now anyone can buy a .net domain name; in fact, it is common for a company to buy all the extensions it can (www.pvlegs.com, www.pvlegs.net, www.pvlegs.info, etc.). Such sites have the same reliability as .com sites.

- **.org** is an abbreviation for organization. Although it is still primarily used by groups, associations, and organizations, it too is now an extension that can be purchased by anyone. Tell students that .org sites may have more expertise behind them than .com sites. For example, they're more likely to find reliable information from www.cancer.org, the website of the American Cancer Society, than from .com sites on the topic of cancer. Caution students that just because an .org site has an organization behind it does not mean the information is neutral or free of bias. The National Rifle Association at www.nra.org, for example, definitely has a message to convey.

- **.gov** is an abbreviation for government, and it truly is restricted to entities of the U.S. federal, state, and local governments. Some .gov sites reflect a political bias (www.whitehouse.gov reflects the opinions of the current president) while others are neutral (www.irs.gov).

- **.edu** is an abbreviation for education, and the extension is reserved for post-secondary institutions and organizations that are accredited by the U.S. Department of Education (colleges, universities, and community colleges). Tell students that the quality of information vetted through an educational website has a higher probability of reliability than something on a .com site.

- **.info** is an extension designed to be used for information websites—sites supposedly designed to be a resource. In actuality, there is no requirement that the registrants of .info domains create something informational in nature. Students should treat these sites with the same caution they use for .com sites.

- **.us**, **.fr**, **.uk**, and **.mx** are examples of country codes (United States, France, United Kingdom, and Mexico). These extensions say nothing about the purpose or quality of the site, so students will have to look elsewhere for clues.

- **.mobi** is a relatively new extension for websites designed to be viewed on mobile devices. The Weather Channel has registered www.weather.com and www.weather.mobi in order to be accessible to people whether they are using a laptop or a smartphone. Visiting a .mobi site will require an extra step of research—namely, to go to the original site in order evaluate its reliability.

Knowing what the domain name communicates about the nature of a site is not the final word on the accuracy or neutrality of its information, but it can greatly improve students' odds of finding good information.

### Teach Wikipedia (6–12)

The Bicholim Conflict is a little-known yet significant war that took place from the middle of 1640 to the early part of 1641. The Portuguese rulers of Goa battled the Maratha Empire for nearly a year. Never heard of it? As I said, it is little known. Why? Well, it's fictitious... and yet an article describing the Bicholim Conflict lived on Wikipedia for five and a half years.

I believe Wikipedia ought to be taught as both a tool and a topic. It's one of the first places students go to when conducting research, and there's little wonder: a Wikipedia article will almost certainly show up on page one of any Internet search. The problem is that few students know what Wikipedia really is or how it works. Here's an explanation in Wikipedia's own words:

> Wikipedia is a multilingual, web-based, free-content encyclopedia project operated by the Wikimedia Foundation and based on an openly editable model.... Wikipedia is written collaboratively by largely anonymous Internet volunteers who write without pay. Anyone with Internet access can write and make changes to Wikipedia articles, except in limited cases. (Wikipedia, n.d.a., ¶1)

In order to prevent vandalism, more and more Wikipedia articles are becoming protected, and in those cases, only registered users can make edits to them. Teach students to beware, regardless. It's true that the information in a Wikipedia article may very well be exceptional: instead of one knowledgeable author presenting information on a topic, potentially thousands of knowledgeable people may have added information and revised the information in the article to correct errors. Author Daniel Pink puts the advantage of Wikipedia this way:

> Instead of clearly delineated lines of authority, Wikipedia depends on radical decentralization and self-organization—open source in its purest form. Most encyclopedias start to fossilize the moment they're printed on a page. But add Wiki software and some helping hands and you get something self-repairing and almost alive. A different production model creates a product that's fluid, fast, fixable, and free. (Pink, 2005, ¶16)

Wikipedia can provide extremely timely information. For example, within minutes of the explosions near the finish line of the Boston Marathon in April 2013, people created an entry and were contributing information. Yet, as the tenure of the Bicholim Conflict entry underscores, the information on Wikipedia may be fraudulent.

There is a smart way to approach this resource, and it's something we can and ought to teach students. The tabs at the top of every article—"Read," "Edit," and "View history"—are usually ignored, but they're the key. In your classroom, fire up Wikipedia, chose an article, and click on the "Edit" tab to show students how easy it is to make a change in an article. Click on the "View history" tab so students can see how frequently the articles are updated. Can we be sure the updates make the article more accurate? No, we can't. Wikipedia cites many studies that have been done assessing Wikipedia's ability to find and fix errors, and other studies that have been done to rate the quality of the articles compared to, say, those in the *Encyclopedia Britannica*. The results are reassuring. But be sure to share with students the words of danah boyd [sic], a principal researcher at Microsoft Research, concerning Wikipedia: "It should be the first source of information, not the last. It should be a site for information exploration, not the definitive source of facts" (2005, ¶1).

## Teach about the tree octopus (6–12)

> The Pacific Northwest tree octopus (*Octopus paxarbolis*) can be found in the temperate rainforests of the Olympic Peninsula on the west coast of North America. Their habitat lies on the Eastern side of the Olympic mountain range, adjacent to Hood Canal. These solitary cephalopods reach an average size (measured from arm-tip to mantle-tip) of 30–33 cm. Unlike most other cephalopods, tree octopuses are amphibious, spending only their early life and the period of their mating season in their ancestral aquatic environment. (Zapato, 2013, ¶1)

So reads the home page of one of the most famous Internet hoaxes. A few years back, researchers from the University of Connecticut asked 25 7th graders to review this website. All 25 students believed that the site was genuine; 24 rated the site as "very credible"; most struggled to find evidence that the website's information was false even after researchers told them that it was. Several stated flat out that they did not believe the Pacific Northwest tree octopus was a hoax (Krane, 2006).

The site, created in 1998 and updated regularly, is brilliantly constructed. There are links, photos, science-y language, videos, faked magazine references, and more. But there are some pretty serious clues that it is an elaborate joke. For starters, Lyle Zapato admits authorship on the bottom of the home page and declares that he is not affiliated "with any school or educational organization other than the Kelvinic University branch of the Wild Haggis Conservation Society."

If you teach students in grade 6 and above, bring your students to this site and work with them to uncover other pieces of evidence that would help reveal the scam. Extend the lesson by encouraging students to be more observant and more skeptical of all the media input they receive.

## Teach students to find the source of online content (6–12)

Many, if not most, websites that are suitable as information sources have an "About" or "About Us" tab—usually on the home page. For years, I had my 8th grade students explore the U.S. national debt as part of my civics instruction. Inevitably, they would find a site with a constantly updating "Debt Clock." There was no "About" tab, but there was a note at the bottom of the page that said the clock was maintained by Ed Hall. Clicking on his name revealed that Ed Hall loved to play with Legos and enjoyed geocaching. While these are interesting hobbies, they don't do much to solidify his credibility as an expert on the U.S. national debt. Year after year, I would explain to my students that Mr. Hall's lack of professional or academic credentials did not mean the information on his site was inaccurate, but it *did* mean that they needed to keep looking for additional information elsewhere. Here are some simple strategies for tracking down source information.

**Truncate.** If students' research takes them to a site with a long URL, suggest that they shorten the address. Cut back to the domain suffix (.com, .net, etc.) where the core site is revealed and "Home" or "About Us" buttons are usually available. So, for example, if www.ascd.org/publications/educational-leadership/apr12/vol69/num07/toc.aspx is the first address, paring back the URL to www.ascd.org will get us to the home page of the site that posted the article.

**Google.** I once handed a book to a student who was researching the topic of the vanishing rainforest. The book was titled *The Vanishing Rain Forest,* which I thought was fairly germane for his topic. What's the first thing this student did? He put the book aside and went to the computer to visit Google.com. Remind students that they can pursue traditional sources of information and avoid sifting through millions of possibly fruitless sites. If they *do* insist on a web search, suggest to students that before they copy the information, they should Google the source. Searching "Lyle Zapato," expert on the Pacific Northwest tree octopus, would have immediately tipped off the 7th graders in the UConn study.

**Look up website owners.** The site www.domaintools.com includes a "Whois" lookup" search box. Type in the web address and you can find the registrant of the site. For example, when I put in www.pvlegs.com, I discovered that the site was registered to someone named Erik Palmer. A subsequent web search revealed that he is an author and consultant. A more dramatic example, one you may already be familiar with, is the site www.martinlutherking.org. Remember that we gave a slight preference to .org sites over .com ones, but this .org site claims, among other things, that Martin Luther King Jr. was a communist, a plagiarist, and an adulterer. Using the Whois tool at www.domaintools.com reveals that the site is registered to Stormfront; a web search of Stormfront identifies the group as a white supremacist community. This is useful information to know.

### Teach Internet reading (6–12)

How do people read online? The easy answer is "They don't!" but that's not really true. We do read online, but we read differently. In his book, *The Shallows,* Nicholas Carr (2011) discusses a number of studies about reading on the web. Among his findings:

> • We read web pages in an *F* pattern: all the way across the top two or three lines, then drop down a bit and read halfway across a couple of lines in the middle of the page, and finally scan down the left edge.

> • We generally spend 19 to 27 seconds on a web page before moving to the next.

> • Our screen-based reading is characterized by "browsing and scanning, keyword spotting, one-time reading, [and] non-linear reading. (p. 135)

Although people today spend more time reading than ever before, this is due to the flood of words on all the digital pages we're constantly viewing. Carr points out that rates of in-depth and concentrated reading are declining.

A prime argument for online textbooks with embedded media and hyperlinks is that words plus video, audio, images, and links to other pages and places provide a much richer learning experience. It's an obvious improvement over the textbook of the past, right? We might believe this intuitively, but research suggests otherwise: "The division of attention demanded by multi-media further strains our cognitive abilities, diminishing our learning and weakening our understanding" (Carr, 2011, p. 135). Why would Emily struggle through the rest of the text about how lightning is created when she can click on a cool video of a great lightning storm? Why would Max read to the bottom of the page when he can click on a hyperlink in paragraph one? (It must have been placed there for a reason, right? Click on it!)

We aren't likely to return to reading habits of the past, and web content creators are not likely to reduce the amount of hypermedia they include on web pages. The cure is to educate students about reading online:

- How the Internet changes reading habits
- How and why to resist hyperlinks
- How web pages are structured and the traps built into them

With middle and high school students, I like to use www.shmoop. com for an Internet reading lesson. Shmoop bills itself as a site for homework help, teacher resources, and test preparation, and at the bottom of the home page they list all the awards they have won from website rating services. Ostensibly, Shmoop is place to go for help with literature, biology, history, Spanish, SAT prep, calculus, and more. I believe it is the place to go to for a demonstration about how dreadful even highly touted informational sites can be.

For starters, notice the ads. Shmoop is free for users, but that means the company must get revenue from somewhere else in order to stay in business. Pop-up video commercials and distracting print ads are the moneymakers. Use these ads as a way to reinforce the commercial aspect of .com sites and discuss with students the importance of staying focused. As Internet readers, we must learn to tune out distractions.

Next, select a topic. When I taught civics, I often chose the Constitution as an example. The Shmoop page on the Constitutional

Convention of 1787 (www.shmoop.com/constitutional-convention/) offers a great lesson about the irrelevance of hyperlinks. I asked students to remember the purpose of our research: to find out how the Constitution was created. Then, in the page's first paragraph of text, I pointed out two hyperlinks: "political" and "social debates." Clicking on the first one took us to an ad for a book by Supreme Court Justice Antonin Scalia; clicking on the second, to an episode of the NPR program *All Things Considered* and a chat with another Supreme Court justice, Stephen Breyer. In the next paragraph was a hyperlink "Bong Hits for Jesus," which took us to a movie review about a movie based on a Supreme Court case. Further down the page, a hyperlink associated with "Justice John Paul Stevens" sent us to his biography at some other website. By now, it was quite clear how absurd hyperlinks can be. Not one of the links led us to an understanding of the Constitutional Convention.

If your school technology specialist will allow it, install an application such as Readability (www.readability.com) on your computers, and suggest to students that they install it on the computers they use at home. Basically, Readability transforms a web page into a "book" page. For example, a web search on Babe Ruth took a student to an About.com page (http://history1900s.about.com/od/people/p/baberuth.htm). At the top of the page was a banner ad for a local food store. The right third of the page was a column with another ad and images from tangentially related videos that the student could click on to watch. Interspersed within the text on the other two-thirds of the page were more ads—for a sports collectible seller, an autograph seller, and someone who claimed to be able to improve a pitcher's fast ball. It was a perfect example of a .com site, and I shared it with the class to reinforce our Internet literacy lessons. Putting the address into Readability turned that page into something you would see in a print biography: text from margin to margin, no ads, and no tangential links.

### Require multiple sources (6–12)

Another one of the activities suggested by Laura, the master teacher and critical skills coach I mentioned earlier, demonstrates to students the importance of using multiple sources for all research projects. To model the process, she pulls together resources all focused on the same topic. For example, there is some debate about schooling's impact on developing creativity. She may find a YouTube video about the Brockhill Park Performing Arts College, an article published in *Newsweek* magazine, an article in *Parenting* magazine, a TED talk by Ken Robinson, a blog by a teacher, and a research article from ERIC. It will become apparent that there are differing views and diverse solutions. She leads students in a discussion. Which source is most credible? Why? Which had the most evidence? Is that necessarily the best source then? Which is most persuasive? Why? What techniques worked to affect your opinion? Students become clear about the need to find multiple sources of input and about the need to apply various tests to evaluate those sources.

Follow that activity with tips for finding multiple sources. Suggest looking for links to additional resources at any site visited. If there are no external links provided, be very suspicious. Students can start at Wikipedia, but if they fail to follow the links at the bottom of the article, they are making a mistake. Any legitimate article will have references at the end. Teach students the importance of pursuing these leads.

### Teach students to use Internet evaluation forms (6–12)

When we assign research papers, we require students to include bibliographies and cite legitimate sources. It's pretty easy to define "legitimate" sources when those sources are traditional print media, such as encyclopedias, scholarly books and journals from established publishers, newspapers, and national magazines. But how do we define, and define for students, what a legitimate online source is? We do that by giving them a guide—a source evaluation form they can use to examine a site's credibility before they invest time reading and taking notes.

Examples of these forms are easy to find online. Students at Naperville North High School in Illinois use the form in Figure 4.3 when they research. Lee Anne, a teacher/librarian at the school, told me that she created the form "because it handles all of the areas

| Figure 4.3 | A Tool for Examining Website Credibility |
|---|---|

**Website Evaluation Form**

Name: _____ Period: _____
Site Name: _____
Site Address/URL

(Respond to the questions below. Leave blank any question that does not apply.)

**Consider WHO is responsible for the website:**
- Does the publisher appear to be knowledgeable about the content?      YES    NO
- Does the publisher qualify as an authority or expert on the topic?      YES    NO
- Can you contact the publisher from the site?      YES    NO
- Is the site's sponsor identified?      YES    NO

**Consider WHAT the content/subject matter of the website is:**
- Does the content appear to be accurate? Error free?      YES    NO
- Is the information presented in an objective manner,
  with a minimum of bias?      YES    NO
- Is there real depth-of-content (vs. information that is
  limited and superficial)?      YES    NO
- Are links from the site appropriate and/or supportive of the content?      YES    NO
- Does the content have educational or informational value?      YES    NO

**Consider WHERE the website resides:**
- What type of domain is this site?      YES    NO
  ___ .gov  ___.com  ___.edu  ___.org  ___.net  ___.biz  ___.mil  ___other
- Is this a personal page with a "~" or ".name" in the URL?      YES    NO

**Consider WHEN the website was last updated:**
- Is the information current?      YES    NO
- Does the site provide information on when it was last updated?      YES    NO
- Does a current date matter?      YES    NO

**Consider HOW the main page looks and functions:**
- Is the page easy to understand and use?      YES    NO
- Is the page well organized?      YES    NO
- Does the page load in a reasonable amount of time?      YES    NO
- Do all of the links work?      YES    NO
- Is the page free from (excessive amounts of) advertising?      YES    NO

**Consider WHY the website exists:**
- Is the site trying to
    sell something?      YES    NO
    inform?      YES    NO
    persuade?      YES    NO
Is the website appropriate for your target audience?      YES    NO
- Is the Internet the best place to find this information
  (vs. books, journals, etc.)?      YES    NO

Conclusion: Is this a good site?
Look over your answers to make your conclusion.      YES    NO

*Source:* Lee Anne Applegate, Naperville Community Unit School District 203, Naperville, Illinois. Used with permission.

that they need to review and consider before using any information found at that particular website for research." The structure of the page—organized by fundamental who, what, where, when, how, and why questions—makes it easy to use. The page asks users to evaluate both the style and substance of the site, addressing multiple aspects of media literacy. Don't send students to the Internet to do research without a similar guiding document.

Let's look back at the anchor standard that began this chapter: **"Integrate and evaluate information presented in diverse media and formats, including visually, quantitatively, and orally."** Now that we have seen what that entails, it is clear that teachers cannot pretend to teach "listening" by hanging up a poster or by occasionally asking students to be quiet (as I once did). It is also clear that students cannot master the skills involved in listening without direct instruction. Something that we currently teach may have to be jettisoned to make room for these new lessons. It is always difficult for teachers to let something go, but the standard may necessitate that. Let me reiterate: it is not the standard that I am most concerned about, but life beyond school. Our students will be woefully unprepared for their digital future without the comprehension lessons we must teach today.

# 5

# QUESTIONING/REASONING

"There are no dumb questions." Although this is something teachers tell students often, I would wager that all of us could tell stories that would prove the adage wrong.

The truth is that students are not innately adept at asking questions. Maybe they believe they understand the content presented by you or a classmate and only later discover that they should have asked a few questions. Occasionally, they don't know what they don't know and have no way to generate questions to elicit clarification. Many struggle to think of the right question at the right time. Similarly, poor reasoning skills can keep students from being able to understand another's point of view or articulate their own, and these deficiencies can lead to miscommunication. Effective questioning and sound reasoning are the foundation of communication and collaboration, and if they are not mastered, successful communication and collaboration will never occur.

## A Look at Standard 3

Standard 3 (SL.3) is the last of the three standards under the Collaboration and Communication heading. Focused on analyzing the information and ideas communicated through speech, its intent is to graduate students who are able to **"evaluate a speaker's point of view, reasoning, and use of evidence and rhetoric."** Here is the grade-level progression:

**Kindergarten:** Ask and answer questions in order to seek help, get information, or clarify something that is not understood.

**Grade 1:** Ask and answer questions about what a speaker says in order to gather *additional* information or clarify something that is not understood.

**Grade 2:** Ask and answer questions about what a speaker says in order to clarify comprehension, gather additional information, *or deepen understanding of a topic or issue.*

In the primary grades, we want students to recognize their own confusion, begin to take action to clarify what they hear, and seek deeper understanding. You'll notice that the language is very similar to Standard 2 at this level. ("Do you have any questions?" "Do you understand why it is important to eat healthy foods?")

**Grade 3:** Ask and answer questions about information from a speaker, *offering appropriate elaboration and detail.*

**Grade 4:** *Identify the reasons and evidence a speaker provides to support particular points.*

**Grade 5:** *Summarize the points a speaker makes and explain how each claim is supported by reasons and evidence.*

In upper elementary, the focus is on finding reasons and evidence. This assumes that listening is confined to the narrow range of informational material and also requires students to be aware of main points and how they are supported. Teachers should ask, "What are the reasons the speaker in the video gives to convince you to exercise more?" "The speaker said we should stop giving kids homework. Was there any proof that homework harms students? What facts proved her point?"

> **Grade 6:** *Delineate a speaker's argument and specific claims, distinguishing claims that are supported by reasons and evidence from claims that are not.*

> **Grade 7:** Delineate a speaker's argument and specific claims, *evaluating the soundness of the reasoning and the relevance and sufficiency of the evidence.*

> **Grade 8:** Delineate a speaker's argument and specific claims, evaluating the soundness of the reasoning and relevance and sufficiency of the evidence *and identifying when irrelevant evidence is introduced.*

Middle grades extend the focus on reasoning and evidence. Students move beyond "What are the reasons?" and "What is the evidence?" to "*How good* are the reasons?" and "*Is there enough* evidence?" This pushes teachers to offer instruction about logic and about evaluating evidence, skills very few students will have at this level. Only *after* we provide this instruction will we be able to ask questions like, "Are those good reasons to ban cell phones at school?" and "Does the number of cell phones in America have anything to do with our school's cell phone ban?"

> **Grades 9–10:** *Evaluate* a speaker's *point of view,* reasoning, and use of evidence *and rhetoric, identifying any fallacious reasoning or exaggerated or distorted evidence.*

> **Grades 11–12:** Evaluate a speaker's point of view, reasoning, and use of evidence and rhetoric, *assessing the stance, premises, links among ideas, word choice, points of emphasis, and tone used.*

We still want high school students to think critically about good reasoning and use of evidence, but now we add awareness of style: it is not just *what* is said but also *how* it is said. Rhetorical devices and delivery techniques are part of listening, and, again, students need direct instruction focused on this content. We cannot ask, "What examples of hyperbole did you notice?" without first teaching the meaning of the word.

There is an obvious and unfortunate limitation in the language of Standard 3: it assumes that the speaker is making an argument in some sort of debate or otherwise attempting to persuade the listener or advance a specific point of view. Yes, listeners should be able to listen for supportive reasons and evidence when presented with an argument, but they should also be prepared to listen to and for much more. Storytelling and humor require well-built messages, too, and we want students to be aware of and able to analyze the techniques associated with those kinds of speech as well. Additionally, those kinds of talks provide variety that engages students. Don't feel the need to limit students to only informational speeches.

## Understanding Argument

It's time to stop and think about what an argument really is. The common usage of the word refers to a verbal disagreement between two people. When a couple is bickering or quarrelling over who has to unload the dishwasher, we might say they are having an argument. That is not how the word is being used when we ask students to "understand a speaker's argument." In that sense of the word, an argument is a series of statements that lead to a logical conclusion. The speaker has a point to make and gives a number of reasons to support that point. (This generally differs from a persuasive speech, which tends to rely on emotion rather than logic. Many a debate has been won by a poorly reasoned but powerfully emotional appeal.)

Most discussions begin when one of the parties states a conclusion—the end statement of some train of thought:

The United States military needs to get out of Afghanistan.

*The Scarlet Letter* should never be taught in school.

Art and PE are important.

A class pet is a good idea.

If we don't have students work backwards to get to the thinking underlying the conclusions, discussions can devolve very quickly:

*Jimmy:* A class pet is a good idea.

*Sally:* No, it isn't. I hate that idea.

*Jimmy:* You're wrong.

*Sally:* Am not.

*Jimmy:* Are too.

*Sally:* Am not.

*Jimmy:* Are too.

Contrast that dead end with the more intelligent discourse here, in which the teacher models the process of asking questions to work backward through a speaker's reasoning:

*Jimmy:* A class pet is a good idea.

*Teacher:* Why do you say that?

*Jimmy:* It is fun to have an animal. Everyone likes pets.

*Teacher:* Is that a good enough reason? Just because it's fun?

*Jimmy:* My dad says taking care of a pet teaches responsibility.

*Teacher:* OK, class. Let's discuss Jimmy's idea. Let's put on the board what he thinks:

1. It is fun to have an animal.

2. Everyone likes pets.

3. Taking care of a pet teaches responsibility.

4. Therefore, we should have a class pet.

Now, let's look at this argument piece by piece. Is the first statement true? Is it fun to have an animal?

*Sally:* It's not fun if you have to clean up after it. My cat always barfs and sometimes doesn't use the litter box, and that's gross. I always get stuck cleaning it up. My mom says it was my idea to get a kitten, so I have to do it.

*Bob:* I love playing fetch with my dog, and she is always excited and fun.

*Tom:* But you can't play fetch with all animals. We had hamsters, and they didn't do anything but run in the dumb wheel.

*Teacher:* So it seems that it is mostly fun *if* you have certain animals. What about Jimmy's next statement: "Everyone likes pets." Does everyone like pets?

*Various students:* Yes!

*Kristen:* Not all pets. I'm allergic to cats. I get a rash and sneeze.

*Greg:* My 4th grade teacher had a snake, and at first we were scared, but everyone loved Pretzel after a while, and we all wanted to hold him.

*Teacher:* And finally, does taking care of a pet teach responsibility?

*Heidi:* Yes, because every morning you have to feed them and stuff.

*William:* I have to clean the dog run once a week, and that's my job. My mom says it's like when I get older and will have a job.

*Teacher:* Well, it looks like this. Some animals are fun. Most of us like having a pet, although it can depend on the kind of pet. Owning a pet does teach us to be responsible. What do you think? Does that make you think we should have a class pet?

In this example, the teacher modeled both questioning and, significantly, how to examine an argument. We don't need to introduce specific terms like *premise* and *conclusion* to younger students; we just need to teach them how to uncover the thinking that led to a speaker's opening statement. With older students, we can teach the specific terminology and require them to produce and challenge evidence. Consider this example:

*Rhonda:* The United States needs to get out of Afghanistan.

*Teacher:* Why do you think that?

*Rhonda:* Because we are spending lots of money on the war, but our country is broke.

*Teacher:* How much money are we spending?

*Rhonda:* Approximately $617 billion.

*Teacher:* Where did you get that number?

*Rhonda:* From costofwar.com.

*Teacher:* And why do you say our country is broke?

*Rhonda:* We are $17 trillion in debt.

*Teacher:* OK, class, who can help us put Rhonda's argument into premises and a conclusion?

Here's how the class's model might look:

1. The war in Afghanistan costs a lot of money. The United States has spent $617 billion on the Afghanistan campaign, according to costofwar.com

2. The United States cannot afford to spend this money because of the national debt, which is $17 trillion.

3. Therefore, the U.S. military should get out of Afghanistan.

I will do much more with this example as we work through the "Take Action" sections of this chapter. Again, the aim is to teach students to think backwards, from conclusions to premises, which is a foundation for solid reasoning. Discussions in which students are merely shouting competing conclusions at each other are a waste of instructional time and, ultimately, go nowhere.

## ⊃ TAKE ACTION: Developing Questioning Skills

The strategies that follow are designed to help students build a basket of skills they can use for various situations in and out of school. Importantly, they force students to think about questioning and reinforce the idea that questioning is a purposeful, thoughtful activity that requires development. The goal is for students to learn which questions to ask and when to ask them.

## Model progressive questioning (K–12)

The grade-level versions of Standard 3 follow a logical progression. We want younger students to ask questions to get clarification and older students to ask questions for analysis. It's a very logical pathway: students need to understand before they can begin to evaluate. Marzano (2013) presents a useful framework for modeling this process in his four levels of questioning:

- *Level 1: Details (K–12)*—asking students to recognize details about information presented. For younger students learning about plants, Level 1 questions might be "What do plants need to live? Why do animals need plants?" Older students learning about HIV might be asked "What are the symptoms of the virus? How do you get the virus? How long does the virus last? How can the virus be treated?" These questions probe for specificity, and at lower grade levels, they are generally all you need to ask.

- *Level 2: Characteristics (3–12)*—asking students to focus on the general category to which Level 1 information belongs. Level 2 questions for the plant topic might be "What are the characteristics of deciduous trees? of coniferous trees?" For the HIV topic, they might be "What are characteristics of all viruses? How does a viral infection differ from a bacterial infection?" Level 2 questions are inferential. If we know how a cold virus behaves and we know how HIV behaves, we can make inferences about viruses in general.

- *Level 3: Elaboration (3–12)*—asking students to elaborate, explain why, describe the effect of, and so on. Sample Level 3 questions might be "Can you tell me more about how desert plants have adapted to the environment? What would happen if the rain forest was cut down?" or "Can you say more about how HIV affects the body? How would an HIV diagnosis change the patient's life? How has HIV changed our lives? What are the societal effects of viruses?" These questions prompt thinking beyond the material directly presented.

- *Level 4: Evidence (4–12)*—asking students to provide support and sources for their elaborations. A prototypical Level 4 question is "On what do you base that answer? Where did you get that idea?" Standard 3 expects students to begin asking these kinds of questions by 4th grade. By 7th grade, they are expected to question the reliability of a speaker's sources ("You based that statement on _____, but is that a reliable source?").

Giving students the knowledge that different kinds of questions elicit different kinds of thinking empowers them to be more effective in their search for understanding.

### Generate a list of question starters (K–12)

Give students a bank of questions and comments that they can use to prompt speakers to elaborate and reveal thought processes, and ask them to them contribute additional starters of their own. As you hear student-generated question-starters used in discussions, add them to the class list. Examples for question-starters for informational talks include

- "Can you explain what you mean by…?"
- "Do you disagree with…?"
- "Is there evidence for…?"
- "Have you considered…?"
- "Why would the author/speaker/expert believe…?"
- "Would you agree that…?"
- "How did you know…?"
- "Would you try to convince us that…?"
- "What would someone on the other side think about…?"

These all pertain to informational talks, of course. But remember that we listen to all kinds of messages: reactions to a novel, personal anecdotes, emotional appeals, and so on. Generate starters for those situations, too:

- "Why would he…"
- "What do you think she was feeling when…"

- "Why did the character decide to…"
- "What would have happened if…"
- "How did the speaker's style contribute to the feeling of…"
- "What do you think we are supposed to feel about…"
- "Have you ever felt like…"

Point out that thoughtful questioning is the way to keep information flowing from a speaker. Whereas a statement of opinion or judgment may cause the speaker to feel defensive and shut down, questioning keeps the conversation moving forward. When getting a speaker to elaborate is the goal, it's often more productive to skip prompts like "You should add some comments about _____" and pose the thought as a question instead: "What if you added some comments about _____?"

## Use "Platonic Seminars" to teach students to ask probing questions (7–12)

Socratic Seminars (sometimes called Socratic Circles) have become quite popular. Unfortunately, most of them have nothing to do with the methods of Socrates. As reported in the dialogues of Plato, Socrates taught by questioning relentlessly and then challenging the responses offered to questions he posed. Socrates never told any speaker that the speaker was wrong or right; instead, he continued to inquire until the speaker came to see the problems in his own reasoning. The Socratic technique requires an extremely strong leader, and yet most guides for setting up Socratic Seminars suggest that the teacher not be a significant participant in the conversation.

Because Socrates's name has been so badly misused, I use Plato's name instead and advocate for "Platonic Seminars." (After all, everything that we know about Socrates comes from Plato's stories about him.) Here's the idea: set up a discussion with a student or small team of students in the role of Socrates. As a proposition is offered, "Socrates" is responsible for asking questions. "Socrates" cannot offer statements of opinion—cannot say, for example, "Yes" or "Good point" or "I disagree"; Socrates can only ask questions. Here's an excerpt of a Platonic Seminar showing the pattern of questioning:

*Sharlene:* I think we need to deport all illegal immigrants.

*Socrates:* How many illegal immigrants are there?

*Sharlene:* About 11 million.

*Socrates:* Do we know how to find all of them?

*Sharlene:* Maybe if we start checking IDs and stuff.

*Socrates:* Wouldn't it take an enormous amount of time and resources for the police to do that?

*Donte:* Probably, yeah.

*Socrates:* Would you rather the police concentrate on stopping violent crime or rounding up illegal immigrants?

*Donte:* Well, stopping crime... but the illegal immigrants are criminals, too.

*Socrates:* Are most of them committing crimes once they are here? Do illegal immigrants contribute to our economy?

*Charles:* I don't think that most of them are breaking laws now. We didn't do research about that, though. I do know they work. Restaurant jobs and hotel cleaning and yard work and picking crops. Low-paying jobs.

*Socrates:* I'm going to assume you're right and they only do low-paying jobs, but doesn't that still contribute to the economy? And if so, who will do those jobs if all of these people are gone?

*Donte:* Well, mostly low-paying jobs, I'm pretty sure. We didn't do any research about that, either. I guess they buy stuff here. And lots of people are unemployed, so the unemployed people could take those jobs.

*Socrates:* Do you want to pick fruit or clean office buildings?

*Sharlene:* Well, *I* don't, but someone might.

As you can tell, "Socrates" has a very difficult job, but if you take a "Team Socrates" approach, letting various students take on the role, you'll see that they can get very good at asking probing questions, especially if they have time for preparation. Platonic Seminars are an excellent way to encourage elaboration, improve understanding, and develop critical thinking.

## Require note taking (4–12)

There are a number of reasons why asking students to write down what they hear is a good idea, but requiring note taking during a discussion has some special benefits. Imagine Aaron, a typical student who tends to quit listening once a speaker's comment has triggered an idea in his head. Aaron's hand shoots up, and all that he can think about is getting a chance to share his idea. Speakers B, C, and D speak before Aaron gets called on. Speaker B made a comment on the same thing that Aaron was thinking, but Aaron was too preoccupied to notice. When Aaron finally gets his turn, some in the class groan because he is making a point they have already heard, and some grin because the comment now seems out of place. Next up is Reynalda, who has also been sitting on a comment triggered by Speaker A. But now she's forgotten what she wanted to say. Both of these scenarios can be avoided by note taking—and I can recommend a very effective structured approach for students to take:

1. Write down the name of every speaker in the discussion.

2. After the speaker's name, record at least one comment that speaker made.

3. If something the speaker says triggers a thought or a question, write that down as well.

For example, here are the notes Lyndsie took during a discussion of whether college athletes should be paid:

> Tamesha: Kid got school free = already paid!
> Reuben: College gets millions from tix
> Hassan: Cant go to Olympics if U R paid
> ME: But Olympic basketball team has pros
> Alicia : Some sports don't sell millions of tix

When Lyndsie gets her chance to contribute to the discussion, she's prepared:

*Lyndsie:* Hassan said that you can't go to the Olympics if you are a pro, but in some sports, like basketball, you can. Then, Reuben, you talked about how much money the schools make on sports, but like Alicia said, there are sports like volleyball and diving that don't bring in as much. Maybe college athletes should get more money when their sport brings in millions, but all of them should get paid, and we should quit pretending that these kids are students.

As Lyndsie speaks, Tamesha adds this to her notes:

Lyndsie: Quit pretending, they are students
ME: What's that mean ?!

I recommend occasionally collecting these notes and looking at them for "with-it-ness" only. Think of them as an ungraded formative assessment that reveals whether or not students are following the discussion and picking up key points.

## Give students process models for analyzing evidence (7–12)

Strong arguments use evidence, but the strength of the evidence matters, too. This means evidence must have relevance; its job is to support the point, not just be related to the same topic. For example, if the point a student is trying to make is that "Smoking is harmful to health," saying, "Twenty-four percent of Japanese adults smoke, but only 16 percent of American adults do" does not advance the argument. That statistic may be true, but it's not relevant.

Lessons about the credibility of Wikipedia and various Internet sources (see Chapter 4) are great springboards for teaching students about various types of evidence, including

• *Statistics/numbers* ("Seventy-three percent of college graduates have some debt.")

- *Facts* ("Water is made up of hydrogen and oxygen.")
- *Examples/individual stories* ("I heard Jae Lin speak perfect English, so it is possible for children born in Asia to master our language.")
- *Expert opinions* ("Ms. Sientis, a professor who has studied stem cells for over 25 years, believes that stem cells will be used to eliminate Alzheimer's disease in our lifetime.")

Be sure to discuss how each type can be used to support a point, modeling that same statement with several kinds of evidence. For example:

*Statement:* Owning a pet is good for your health.

*Statistic:* People who never owned a cat are 40 percent more likely to die of a heart attack than people who have owned a cat.

*Fact:* A study shows that petting a cat lowers blood pressure.

*Example:* My neighbor is 98 years old and has always had pets.

*Expert:* Bob Vetere, president of the Human Animal Bond Research Initiative Foundation, says human health is positively affected by pet ownership.

With older students, model how to evaluate evidence. Let's use Rhonda's comments earlier in this chapter to demonstrate how a teacher might prompt critical thinking about evidence:

*Teacher:* Rhonda, do you have any evidence? Any idea how much the government has spent in Afghanistan or how much in debt the United States is?

*Rhonda:* Yeah, I did some research. We have spent $617 billion so far in Afghanistan but we are $17 trillion in debt. We can't afford it.

*Teacher:* OK, let's look at Rhonda's support. The war has cost $617 billion. *Is* that a lot? How much does the federal government spend each year? What could that money be used for instead? What have we gotten for the money that has been spent there? Does the cost of the war alone support Rhonda's point?

[Pause for discussion]

*Teacher:* Rhonda also said the nation has a $17 trillion debt. Why is that an important number? Is debt bad? Why or why not? Is there an acceptable amount of debt? How do we know how much is too much? Class, your thoughts?

[Pause for discussion]

*Teacher:* Finally, let's examine the reliability of the evidence. Tell us again where you got your information, Rhonda?

*Rhonda:* From www.costofwar.com and from www.brillig.com.

*Teacher:* So what do we know about these sites? Who is behind Cost of War? What is Brillig? Are there other sites that can verify these numbers?

With this knowledge and these models, students can become adept at examining the support for statements and critically evaluating information they receive.

## ⊃ TAKE ACTION: Developing Reasoning Skills

Soundness of reasoning, relevance of evidence, sufficiency of evidence, identifying fallacies, evaluating rhetoric—these are all expectations of Standard 3, and all of them ask students to think about the messages they receive. The strategies that follow provide students with the tools needed to do that strong, analytical thinking.

### Teach logic (6–12)

Formal logic is a branch of mathematics that is seldom taught, but it is extremely helpful when it comes to developing students' ability to analyze arguments. The first simple step in teaching logic is to introduce three key concepts: *induction, deduction,* and *syllogism.*

*Induction* (inducing) means moving from specifics to a general conclusion. It's a staple of crime shows. ("Mr. X was near the scene of the crime at the time; he owned the type of gun that fires the bullets found; his fingerprints were found on the door; he bought a new car a day later. Therefore, Mr. X was the one who robbed the store.")

*Deduction* (deducing) is the reverse: moving from a general statement to a specific one. ("The dogs always bark when they see a stranger. The dogs didn't bark when the computer was stolen, so the person who took the computer must not have been a stranger.")

A *syllogism* is common type of deductive argument—and the most commonly used method of argument. Syllogisms have three parts: (1) a general observation, (2) a specific observation, and (3) a conclusion. Here's the classic example:

> All men are mortal.
> Socrates is a man.
> Therefore, Socrates is mortal.

For a syllogism to work, two things must be true: the statements must logically lead to the conclusion, and each statement must be true. Here's an example of a syllogism that fails the first condition:

> Jim is hungry.
> Jim is American.
> Therefore, all Americans are hungry.

Both statements about Jim are true, but they don't support the conclusion. Here's a syllogism that fails the second condition:

> Americans are fat.
> Jim is an American.
> Therefore, Jim is fat.

Now it's the first statement that's not true. It is not the case that all Americans are fat, so the argument breaks down.

In this brief overview, I've used the formal terms, but I encourage you to introduce these logical reasoning concepts in grade-appropriate language. Under the Common Core, by the time students reach upper elementary school, they should be able to "identify the reasons and evidence a speaker gives to support points" (4th grade) and "explain how a speaker's claims are supported by reasons and evidence" (5th grade). By middle school, they must show that they can evaluate those reasons and evidence. There's no need to ask 6th graders to tell you which premise of the syllogism is problematic, but you might say, "Her point is based on two statements. Can you identify the two statements that lead to her conclusion? Do you agree with those two statements? Which one bothers you? Why does it bother you?" A 6th grader could be expected to generate responses like these:

> *Sonia:* I think the point is wrong, because one of the statements is wrong—it isn't true. "Ice caps are melting"—that statement is true, but we don't have the proof that "humans caused the ice caps to melt," so I can't agree that humans can fix it.

> *Maggie:* I think the conclusion is wrong, because it doesn't add up. Yes, some school lunches have a lot of fat and calories, and yes, some kids are obese, but that doesn't mean school lunches cause obesity. There are other things going on.

Let's go back to Rhonda again. That discussion could come out this way:

> *Teacher:* Class, I think we can state Rhonda's argument this way. Premise 1: *The war in Afghanistan has cost a lot of money.* Premise 2: *The United States is in debt.* Conclusion: *Therefore, the United States should get out of Afghanistan.* Let's ask first if this is a good argument. With a strong argument, there is no way a reasonable person can avoid coming to the same conclusion. So does this argument add up? If the war costs a lot of money, and if the United States is in debt, does that compel us to believe that we should get out of Afghanistan?

At the point, the teacher can prompt the class with various questions: Is money the only factor? If the United States spends some now, will it save more later? Are there "expenses" besides monetary ones? The goal is to get the class to consider whether agreement is compelled by the argument.

### Teach reasoning errors (4–12)

An important step in developing students' reasoning skills is teaching them about what logicians call *fallacies*. In the lower grades, we might just call them "bad reasoning" or "poor thinking." Here are the types of fallacies students need to know and can grasp even at young ages:

- *Attacking the person*—saying something personal instead of something against the content. ("Of course you are for gun control because you are a vegetarian nutcase.")
- *Circular reasoning*—using your support as your main point, also known as begging the question. ("Healthy foods will improve your overall health because good food is good for you.")
- *Cause versus correlation*—thinking that because two things happened or two conditions exist at the same time, one must have caused the other. ("He ate a hamburger right before he robbed that store. We should ban hamburgers because they cause crime.") Stress that sometimes there may be a causal link, but it can't be proven from the statement. The fact that someone played Grand Theft Auto right before stealing a car does not mean that playing the game caused the crime or influenced the thief's decision to commit the crime, but it can't be ruled out, either.
- *Derailing*—purposefully changing the point to come up with something easier to argue. ("I don't want to put my child in a car seat because car seats aren't a big deal and the government has no right to tell me what to do." From this point, the discussion can easily turn to an argument over the government's right to regulate behavior, when the topic is simply "Are car seats a good idea?")
- *Posing a fake argument*—misstating an opposing view to make it look worse. ("He wants to limit the websites viewable in school because he is against technology.")
- *Distracting with emotion*—deliberately diverting the listener's attention from the issue by making an emotional appeal. ("He didn't

do his homework, but it wasn't his fault. Could you do homework if you didn't have dinner? If your parents were never home? If you felt lonely? If no one seemed to care about you at all?")

• *Changing the burden of proof*—forcing the other side to disprove your point. ("I say that video games cause gun violence. Can you prove that they don't?")

• *Generalizing*—taking one example and making a general statement. ("I was in Paris for a week, and I can tell you, France has lousy weather.")

• *Either/or*—suggesting that there are only two possibilities. ("Either quit drinking soda or develop diabetes.")

• *Ignoring some facts*—selecting certain facts that support a point while ignoring others. ("Americans watch violent movies, and we have high murder rates." OK, but Japanese watch as many violent movies, and Japan doesn't have high murder rates.)

• *Prejudice/stereotypes*—making arguments based on personal bias. ("Student athletes focus on sports because they aren't smart enough to succeed in class.")

It will be easier for students to evaluate the relevance of a speaker's reasoning if they are familiar with some of these common reasoning errors. Introduce these as appropriate for your students.

## Teach persuasive techniques (4–12)

In order for students evaluate the soundness of a speaker's reasoning, the relevance of supporting points, and the speaker's use of rhetoric, we need to teach them the common rhetorical tricks designed to persuade. Whether selling soap, a smartphone, or an argument, speakers use certain time-tested ways to convince an audience to buy or believe. Introduce some of the main techniques:

• *Testimonial*—an endorsement by a famous person. If a star athlete or entertainment figure says it's true, that has persuasive power over some people.

• *Plain folks*—referencing ordinary people that the target market can identify with to increase their comfort with an idea. ("Joe the Plumber" said John McCain was a good choice for president. If you are a regular person, then John McCain must be a good choice for you, too.)

• *Bandwagon*—communicating that everyone else is doing or believing *X*, and audience members who want to be socially acceptable and popular should do or believe *X* as well.

• *Fear*—presenting a scary situation and then giving the audience a way to feel safe. ("Terrorists are everywhere and our borders are porous. Only by electing _____ can this be solved.")

• *Transference*—surrounding the product, person, or idea with things that make people feel good (puppies, babies, farms, grandparents, cultural symbols). The idea is that the audience will transfer these good feelings to the product, person, or idea. Ever notice how often U.S. political candidates speak while standing in front of an American flag?

• *Repetition*—repeating short phrases to cement a point or bias the listener. ("Bully-proofing works because it changes our thinking. Bully-proofing works because it changes our behavior. Bully-proofing works because our schools are safer. Bully-proofing works.")

• *Statistic without context*—providing facts and figures that seem to prove the point without any follow-up in the hope that the audience will accept these facts and figures at face value. ("Using corn to produce ethanol can cut greenhouse gas emissions by 52 percent!" "Sixty percent of people on Earth are malnourished, and using corn for fuel makes the problem worse!")

• *Loaded words*—incorporating words known to have a powerful emotional impact. Consider how the use of terms like *fascist, tree-hugger, liberal, redneck, nerd, jock, prep,* and *skater* resonate with different audiences.

Making students aware of these techniques and giving them practice spotting examples can help them resist rhetoric and concentrate on the ideas. However, be sure to stress that using one of these persuasive tricks does not mean the speaker's core message is invalid. What it does mean is that the speaker is trying to influence and manipulate the audience, as all good salespeople do, whether they are selling a product or an idea.

### Teach rhetorical devices (8–12)

Notice that I used the word *rhetorical* in the previous strategy as well. Certainly there is an overlap between that strategy and this one, but I think there is enough of a distinction to make teaching rhetorical devices its own strategy. The aim here is to show older students how effective speakers improve their message with specific stylistic additions:

- *Allusion*—a reference to some other person, event, book, film, or the like. "President Reagan was not Superman, but the way he dealt with Russia was amazing" sneakily gets us associating Reagan with a superhero.
- *Analogy*—a comparison of two different things. "Hitler almost destroyed civilization, and if we don't stop Saddam Hussein, he might destroy the world, too" makes Hussein seem much worse than he might have if not linked in such a way.
- *Hyperbole*—a gross exaggeration. "A child is exposed to advertising for unhealthy foods thousands of times a day" makes the problem seem much bigger than it is.
- *Parallel structure*—using similar phrases to emphasize points. Martin Luther King Jr.'s speech is perhaps the most famous example of this, repeating "And I have a dream that…".
- *Alliteration*—using words that begin with the same consonant. "They have been bullied, beaten, and battered by unfair treatment" is a more powerful and memorable message than "They have been bullied, pushed around, and treated unfairly."

Encourage students in grades 8–12 to look for other devices and examples of their occurrence.

An exploration of the Common Core's set of "listening standards" turns out to be an exercise in expanding the definition of listening. After starting with the simple asking and answering of questions to get information, we've now looked at logic, rhetoric, reasoning, and more. Halfway through the standards, we have come a long way.

There are great challenges for teachers. We have to change instruction—and, yes, some old favorite lessons may need to give way to more important material. But remember that you don't have to teach all of these skills by yourself. For example, you might commit to teaching persuasive techniques and have a teammate commit to teaching active listening. Just make sure that, somehow, all students receive instruction they must have in order to master comprehension and collaboration.

# 6

# SPEAKING WELL

The vast majority of our communication is oral. Most of our students will be asked to speak face to face with a variety of audiences: classmates now, and some day co-workers, clients, team members, staff, and many others. Living in a world of digital communication devices and websites means some of our students will be called on to create videos, webinars, and podcasts. All of them will be likely be using FaceTime, Skype, and the replacements that will eventually make those particular products obsolete.

Occasionally asking students to come up to the front of the room and give a talk will not prepare them to meet the speaking demands of the world they live in. The question becomes "How can we prepare them?" And to know that, we have to ask and answer another question: just what is effective speaking?

Let's work this out. Think of some time in your life when you heard a great speaker, someone who really impressed you. Now imagine that right after the speech, someone asked you what you thought. Imagine the conversation.

*You:* That was amazing. That speaker is one of the best I have ever heard.

*Someone:* Why do you say that? What was so good about him?

*You:* His grammar! He had *amazing grammar.*

Probably not, right? So what was it then? Was it the speaker's carefully selected supporting details? Was it his use and citation of resources? The well-designed transitions? Was it the impressive figurative language or the precise use of technical language? These are certainly things speakers must think about ahead of time as part of what I have called "building a speech" (Palmer, 2011). They are also instantly recognizable as components of good writing, and there are definitely strong parallels between effective *written* messages and effective *spoken* messages. And yet, communicating to listeners rather than readers requires something more, something different. All of us have had the experience of sitting in a conference hall and listening to a speaker read a well-written essay, and I'll bet all of us were bored by the recitation. So while supporting details, deft transitions, and well-chosen language factor into effective speaking, they are not what defines it.

Think back again to that great speaker, one of the best you've ever heard. I'm guessing that the largest part of what impressed you was what the speaker did *as he was speaking*, what I have referred to as "performing a speech" (Palmer, 2011). The performing talent is very different than the building talent. We do not give an actress an Academy Award because the lines she delivers were so well written. Of course the lines are important, but in the world of oral communication, the speaker who impresses does so by *performance* more than by words. If we really want to develop competent speakers, we need to give much more thought to delivery than speaking standards typically recommend. In this chapter, we'll explore how to create instruction that addresses both aspects of speaking well.

How does the Common Core's Speaking and Listening Standard 4 measure up as a guide for effective speaking instruction? Let's take a look and find out.

## A Look at Standard 4

Standard 4 (SL.4) introduces us to the second topic of the Common Core's Speaking and Listening standards: "Presentation of Knowledge and Ideas." Here, the specific focus is speaking well: the content and delivery of student talk, including reports and presentations. The ultimate aim is to produce graduates who can **"present information, findings, and supporting evidence such that listeners can follow the line of reasoning and the organization, development, and style are appropriate to task, purpose, and audience."** Here is the grade-level progression of Standard 4:

> **Kindergarten:** Describe familiar people, places, things, and events and, with prompting and support, provide additional detail.

> **Grade 1:** Describe people, places, things, and events with *relevant details, expressing ideas and feelings clearly.*

> **Grade 2:** *Tell a story or recount an experience with appropriate facts* and relevant, descriptive details, *speaking audibly in coherent sentences.*

In the primary grades, the focus is squarely on content. It's about *what* is said rather than *how* it is said. Students are asked to tell about personal experiences and to include important details. In grade 2, we see the first, very minimal direction about *how* to speak: students must speak loudly enough to be heard.

> **Grade 3:** *Report on a topic or text,* tell a story, or recount an experience with appropriate facts and relevant, descriptive details, speaking *clearly at an understandable pace.*

> **Grade 4:** Report on a topic or text, tell a story, or recount an experience in an organized manner, using appropriate facts and relevant, descriptive details *to support main ideas or themes;* speak clearly at an understandable pace.

> **Grade 5:** Report on a topic or text *or present an opinion, sequencing ideas logically and* using appropriate facts and relevant, descriptive details to support main ideas or themes; speak clearly at an understandable pace.

In upper elementary, the content of the talk continues to get the most attention. In addition to talking about personal experiences, students should be able to "report" on text. They move from adding details to adding fact. Additionally, there's another element of building a speech to address: organization. Students must put information in logical order. Still, there is almost no consideration about how to deliver the talk, although the "be audible" requirement becomes a bit more specific in that it addresses enunciation and speed.

**Grade 6:** *Present claims and findings,* sequencing ideas logically and using pertinent *descriptions,* facts, and details *to accentuate main ideas or themes; use appropriate eye contact, adequate volume, and clear pronunciation.*

**Grade 7:** Present claims and findings, *emphasizing salient points in a focused, coherent manner* with pertinent descriptions, facts, details, and examples; use appropriate eye contact, adequate volume, and clear pronunciation.

**Grade 8:** Present claims and findings, emphasizing salient points in a focused, coherent manner with *relevant evidence, sound valid reasoning, and well-chosen* details; use appropriate eye contact, adequate volume, and clear pronunciation.

When students reach middle school, the personal stories are gone; Standard 4 is now concerned with informational speeches only. But the standard in these grades continues to emphasize how a speech is built over how it is delivered, and content and organization are dominant. Middle school speakers are expected to include details, facts, examples, and, in 8th grade, evidence and reasoning. "Logical sequencing" becomes "focused, coherent manner," but that language change is insignificant. The basic notion remains that the speech must be well organized. The only new delivery requirement is the addition of eye contact.

**Grades 9–10:** Present *information,* findings, and supporting evidence *clearly, concisely, and logically such that listeners can follow the line of* reasoning and the *organization, development, substance, and style are appropriate to purpose, audience, and task.*

**Grades 11–12:** Present information, findings, and supporting evidence, *conveying a clear and distinct perspective,* such that listeners can follow the line of reasoning, *alternative or opposing perspectives are addressed,* and the organization, development, substance, and style are appropriate to purpose, audience, and a *range of formal and informal* tasks.

By high school, almost all of the emphasis is on building the speech. Still informational only, still concerned with adequate evidence and reasoning, and still concerned with logical organization, in the high school grades, Standard 4 adds that the speech has to be built with a particular audience in mind (entailing adjusting substance and formality) and by 11th and 12th grades, built to include distinct perspectives. There are no guidelines about how to deliver the message.

Now, let's explicitly separate the "building" pieces of Standard 4 from the "performing" pieces—separate what students must do *before delivering* a report or presentation from what they must do *during the delivery* (see Figure 6.1). It's a division we can use to guide our instruction.

## Understanding Message Building

In my book *Well Spoken* (Palmer, 2011), I describe the five things effective speakers do before they ever say a word. Two of these are addressed in Standard 4: content and organization.

### Content

What makes up the content of an oral presentation? The language of the grade-level versions of Standard 4 gives us some guidance: *describe people, places, things, events; tell a story; give a report; and present findings.* Notice that the content is almost all informational. This is an unfortunate limitation. I encourage you to stress that presenting "information, findings, and supporting evidence" is important but to let students know that a competent speaker can also tell a great story. We will talk more about that in Chapter 8.

| Figure 6.1 | "Building" and "Performing" Components of Standard 4 by Grade Level | |
|---|---|---|
| Grade | Building | Performing |
| K | describe places; provide detail | |
| 1 | describe places; relevant details | clearly |
| 2 | tell a story with facts; relevant descriptive details, coherent sentences | audibly |
| 3 | … facts, relevant descriptive details | clearly; understandable pace |
| 4 | … organized manner; facts, relevant descriptive details | clearly; understandable pace |
| 5 | … sequencing logically; facts, relevant descriptive details | clearly; understandable pace |
| 6 | … sequencing logically; facts, relevant descriptive details | eye contact; adequate volume; clear pronunciation |
| 7 | … focused, coherent manner; pertinent descriptions, facts, details, examples | eye contact; adequate volume; clear pronunciation |
| 8 | … focused, coherent manner; evidence, reasoning, details | eye contact; adequate volume; clear pronunciation |
| 9–10 | … information, evidence; concisely, logically such that listeners can follow the organization, development, substance | style appropriate to purpose |
| 11–12 | … information, evidence, opposing perspectives; such that listeners can follow the organization, development, substance | style appropriate to purpose |

What additional content is needed? From the primary grades on, Standard 4 stresses facts and details, and when students reach 8th grade, they are expected to incorporate evidence. Facts, details, and evidence are exactly what teachers stress in writing instruction. It should be no stretch for us to meet this part of the standard, and in doing so, we'll also be supporting students' mastery of writing standards. If a student wrote a paragraph that said, "I believe that we need more security at school," and wrote nothing further, the teacher would certainly comment, "Why? What kind of security? Is there a problem? Do you have examples?" We shouldn't have lower expectations for oral assignments.

In English and language arts classrooms, teachers spend a lot of time asking students to add details. Because writing instruction has traditionally focused on writing fiction, asking for details is associated with asking students to make the scene more vivid or say more about a character's motivation. As we transition to more non-fiction writing, and as content-area teachers begin to incorporate writing instruction into their assignments, we need to get into the habit of asking students to back up their assertions and provide support for their opinions.

That said, if a student built a speech with facts, details, examples, and evidence, would that be sufficient to engage listeners? Of course not. Imagine listening to this speech:

> *Amin:* Hi, my name is Amin, and I will tell you about climate change. Ice caps are melting. Last year, 60 percent of the Arctic ice cap melted, which is the largest amount in the last 150 years. Glaciers are melting. Over half of Switzerland's glaciers have disappeared in the last 30 years. Droughts are increasing. Seventy percent of the United States experienced a drought last year. Thank you for listening.

Main points? Check. Each with a relevant example and evidence? Check and check. But something is missing, isn't it? Amin met the content requirements but failed to create an effective speech. What went wrong?

Simply put, the content requirements here are incomplete. There is much more to an effective spoken presentation than information in the form of main ideas with supporting details and evidence. When we think of presentation content, we must also consider a grabber opening, clarifying information, connectors, and a powerful closing (Palmer, 2011, 2012). This means Amin should engage the audience immediately with an opening that hooks them. He should clarify some things about the Arctic ice cap. (He studied the topic, but his audience did not. He knows what the Arctic ice cap is, but do they? What *is* the Arctic ice cap? Why does it matter if it melts? Switzerland has glaciers? Is that important?) Amin also needs to connect his topic to his audience. Random facts have no impact. The question listeners want answered is "Why should *I* care?" And Amin needs to finish with some statement that has an impact—that leaves the audience with something to think about or do.

Here's what a section of Amin's speech might look like with expanded content expectations:

> *Amin:* ... Our planet is heating up. In fact, it is dangerously overheating, and enormous problems will occur in your lifetime. Ice caps are melting. At the North Pole, the Arctic Ocean is a frozen ice shelf. It provides a home to polar bears, and it is a major source of cool air that blows around the globe, keeping temperatures livable. The food you eat cannot grow if temperatures get too high, so all of us depend on that cool air. Last year, 60 percent of the Arctic ice cap melted, the largest amount in the last 150 years.... It's very simple: either we act now or we watch life as we know it die. You decide.

We have been expecting too little of our students. If we specifically teach them how to add to the minimal content we usually require, we can get exceptional talks instead of mediocre ones (Palmer, 2011). Of all of the Common Core's Speaking and Listening standards, I think Standard 4 is by far the weakest. By requiring only the barest content elements, it fails to require students to add elements that make talks engaging and compelling. You will want to encourage your students to do more.

## Organization

After presenting main ideas, adding adequate detail or evidence, and including the other keys to effective content, the content must be organized. Standard 4 has this expectation covered.

Notice the language in the grade-level versions: "in an organized manner," "by sequencing logically," "in a focused, coherent manner," and "such that listeners can follow the organization." This is a very left-brained approach to building a presentation, and you may wonder if students shouldn't be free to use a less rigid approach to organizing their thoughts. After all, we have all read novels and seen films and television programs that are engaging and understandable in spite of illogical time shifts and seemingly haphazard transitions. Couldn't some student, for example, give an entertaining talk about *A Wrinkle in Time* with random, out-of-order scenes from the novel? Probably, but it's worth remembering that Picasso mastered life drawing before he moved into new territory. I think we are wise to begin with a formulaic approach, especially in the lower grades. Just put things in logical order. Use chronological order to tell the story. When presenting information, provide the fact and then the details and evidence for that fact.

Arguably, high school students could be a little less organizationally restricted. Standard 4 is careful to point out that in grades 9–12, organization and style should be appropriate to the task and audience. If the style needed to design a particular message for a particular audience allowed it, a time-shifting presentation might be appropriate. For example, the novel *Slaughterhouse-Five* is chronologically disorganized, but high school students understand it, and a presentation on this novel could certainly justify a similar organizational approach.

## ⮑ TAKE ACTION: Developing Message-Building Skills

To reiterate, all speaking involves two very different skills, *constructing* the talk and *delivering* the talk. This section covers strategies to help student speakers do what they have to do before they ever open their mouths.

Teachers are generally quite explicit about what they want in a presentation. We ask students to include the main character, plot, and setting; the name of the biome and the plants and animals in it; and so on. What I suggest here are some simple things that we too easily overlook when we give speaking assignments but that go a long way when it comes to helping students build a good speech.

## Stress the need to use real language (4–12)

No talk is improved by adding big words or odd phrases. Whether we are talking to one person, several, or many, a conversational tone is best. Yes, it may be necessary to converse in the style of the audience (see Chapter 8), but what's said should be free of fillers, jargon, and thesaurus discoveries.

Show students some hypothetical examples. If you teach high school, you might ask your students to imagine they are being interviewed by the selection committee of a major university. They've been asked to present their qualifications. How should they reply? In their normal style of speech?

> *Student:* I'm all, like, totally qualified, because I got, like, really good grades and test scores and everything like that.

Or would it be better to use language that's fancy and "formal"?

> *Student:* I believe that my academic qualifications are superlative in that I have heretofore received adequate to above-average marks from my instructors as well as college placement exam scores that, in comparison to the scores of many of my peers, are beyond the norm.

Neither of those would be appropriate. Point out that formal language does not mean unnecessary phrases; big audiences and big stakes do not mean we need big words. How about this?

> *Student:* I believe I am qualified because my grade point average and my test scores are both above the averages of students applying to this school.

During these illustrations, be sure to solicit student input on "how else they might say it." Ask students to look for examples of poorly worded and well-worded writing and speaking. Post "Eschew obfuscation" on the board as a reminder to be careful.

### Ask students to be specific and concrete (4–12)

Readers of an essay can reread any part they don't understand, but listeners do not have that option. There is no rewind button for the class discussion, the comments during group work, or the in-class presentation. For this reason, students must focus on making their speech clear. Generalities are not helpful. Vagueness is undesirable. Share examples to drive the point home:

> *Student:* There are many ways that we could improve our schools. Some of the changes have to do with respect. Lots of us can change common behaviors that would make daily things more comfortable.

This is better:

> *Student:* We can make our school better by respecting one another. Walk in the hallways. Keep moving. Keep your voices down. Pick up after yourself.

It is consistent with Standard 4's expectations to add detail and offer some examples. Collect actual student examples for use with subsequent classes.

> *Teacher:* Last year, a student in this health class gave a speech about unhealthy foods. He said, "Bad foods can cause heart problems." How might he have made that more specific and detailed?
>
> *Brianna:* He could have said what bad foods are. What is a bad food? A fried food?

### Use organizers (K–12)

Graphic and other kinds of content organizers can help students at all grade levels structure their speaking in a straightforward logical or chronological way. For example, have students make a timeline and fill in the story they want to tell or the event they want to explain in terms of how it began, what happened next, and so on. Create an outline with main points, reasons/evidence, and details and ask them to use it when writing or revising a speech. There are many online sources for these kinds of organizers, among them ReadWriteThink (www.readwritethink.org) created by the International Reading Association and National Council of Teachers of English, where you can download dozens of organizers—a Persuasion Map, a Making Connections Chart, and a Sequence of Events Chart to name a few. Many of these organizers are designed to help students tackle different genres of writing. Yes, I said *writing*. We touched on the speaking/writing connection back at the beginning of this chapter, noting that the process of building a speech is a writing process. It's only logical that organizers that aid writing can aid speech preparation.

### Provide a Thinking Map (6–12)

The multi-flow map format (see Figure 6.2) is a good tool for encouraging the kind of thinking necessary to develop a strong written or oral argument.

This is one of eight kinds of "maps" created by Thinking Maps Inc. (see www.thinkingmaps.com). Each is designed to be a visual representation of a particular thought process, and a multi-flow map is designed to model cause-and-effect thinking. Recall that most discussions begin with a conclusion and proceed to uncover the reasons behind that conclusion. The middle area of the multi-flow map is the statement of the conclusion. Circles (or boxes) on the left are statements that might cause someone to arrive at the conclusion; circles or boxes on the right are statements of effects that would result from the conclusion. The value of this map is that it prompts students to look at both sides: the compelling reasons for a proposition and the negative consequences that may actually outweigh the reasons and lead students to rethink the position.

| Figure 6.2 | A Multi-Flow Thinking Map for Considering Cause and Effect |
|---|---|

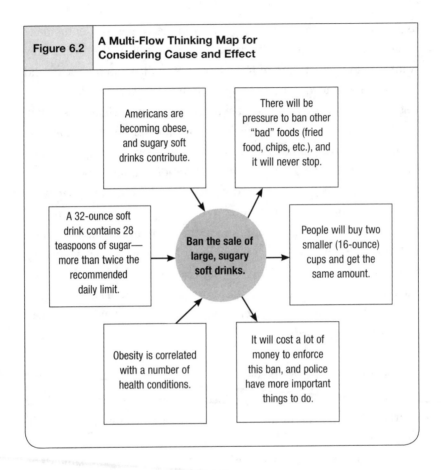

## Understanding Delivery

As noted, when it comes to good speaking, building a message is only part of the battle. When we give a *speaking* assignment, we ought to give a lot of weight to performance, or how well students do the actual speaking.

I am wary of oral presentation rubrics that focus too much on message construction and too little on message delivery. For example, a rubric may offer 10 points for including main ideas, 10 points for presence of supporting details, 10 points for use of citations, 10 points for organization, and 10 points for delivery. A student who constructed the speech well could easily get 80 percent of the possible points; if she can mumble the words and pick up just a couple of points in the delivery category, she might technically be called "proficient." This is a mistake. (As we shall see in Chapter 9, the Smarter Balanced Assessment Consortium, which will be assessing mastery of the Common Core standards, makes this mistake as well.) Again, think back to that great speaker you remember; it's delivery that tends to impress most. Effective communicators understand that good speaking is more than merely verbalizing well-constructed writing.

### What We Look For

So what does it take to "perform" well-written words? Look back at Figure 6.1 (p. 111), with its breakdown of Standard 4's message-building and message-performing components. Ask yourself if the descriptors in the "Performing" column are sufficient. For example, the performance expectation for a 2nd grader is just to speak audibly. It suggests that a wiggly student constantly tugging at his sleeve, looking at the floor, and speaking monotonously, quickly, and without gestures would meet the standard as long as he spoke audibly.

Turning to the performance expectations of the secondary grades now, if a middle school student spoke with adequate volume, used clear pronunciation, and made eye contact, would that really be sufficient? What about shuffling feet, playing with hair, and speaking monotonously, quickly, and without gestures? By high school, the only suggestion of what is required is an "appropriate style." What does that mean? What does that include? Imagine telling students, "Please use an appropriate style." Imagine the blank or quizzical looks you'd get.

When I ask teachers in my workshops to describe the characteristics of an effective speaker, the question usually elicits an awkward pause and a roomful of faces conveying the thought "We were never trained in this." I follow up by asking the teachers to call out the performance or delivery-related words on their speaking rubrics. Here's a sampling of the wide assortment these rubrics provide: *intonation, elocution, articulation, inflection, expression, enthusiasm, loudly, pitch, rhythm, clearly, slowly, volume, hold head up, body language, posture, tone, eye contact, poise, look at audience, stand up straight, gestures, projection, body movement, enunciation, presence, fluid expression, confidence, interesting voice,* and *vocal modulation.*

Let's look at these characteristics critically. First, are they clear? Would students in any grade level understand what *vocal modulation* is? I also wonder if *intonation, fluid expression* (as opposed to just *expression*), and *presence* convey anything of value to students.

> *Teacher:* Miranda, you had expression in that presentation, but it wasn't fluid enough. Please also work on modulating your voice and add some intonation.

How helpful is this feedback? Would Miranda be able to understand, self-correct, and give a better presentation the next time? I assume that we all agree that no skill should be scored on a rubric unless it's something you have explicitly taught and given students lots of practice mastering. I would certainly be interested to see the lessons that are used to teach abstruse concepts like *presence:*

> *Teacher:* Class, when you present next week, I will score you on presence. Today, I want to teach you how to have presence, and we will have several practice activities that focus on presence. Presence means that you have a stately or distinguished bearing. Now, watch me as I demonstrate distinguished carriage.

Many of the terms on the list of performance traits my workshop attendees generate from their rubrics are flat-out bad advice. As an example, I often see "Speak loudly, clearly, and slowly" on rubrics. First, speaking loudly is annoying and unnecessary. I assume the intention is to let students know that we need to hear every word, but "speak loudly" is a poor way to phrase that. A quiet voice can be very powerful. Yes, every word needs to be heard, but speaking loudly is often inappropriate.

"Speak slowly" is equally misguided as blanket advice. When you are recounting the exciting play that ended in your team scoring the winning goal, you need a quick pace. Go ahead and read the following passage out loud, first slowly and then again, but now speed up the tempo to reproduce the excitement of the game's pivotal moment:

> The defender slipped slightly. I quickly pushed the ball past him and raced to the goal. Two other defenders came rushing at me. The keeper's eyes lit up. I fired off a shot just as the defenders converged on where the ball had been. Too late!

Rather than "speak slowly," what students need to do is learn to pay attention to the speed of their speech and practice adjusting it for effect.

Another frequently appearing performance requirement I'd like to challenge? *Rhythm.*

> *You would really think it odd if I had rhythm in my speech;*
> *Though very good for birthday cards, it's not something to teach.*

I also disagree that students need *enthusiasm* in their speeches. Should a speaker be enthusiastic about the fact that almost one billion people on this planet go to sleep hungry every night? Should the story that ends in the dog's death be told with enthusiasm? (Only if the dog has been terrorizing the town, I think.) Again, speaking with *enthusiasm* is a poor way of phrasing what we want students to avoid, which is speaking monotonously.

Look back at the list of terms on pages 119–120. Some of the performance descriptors that seemed acceptable, commonplace, and innocuous now just might strike you as questionable.

### Multiple-Trait Speaking

Many years ago, I noticed that my students' presentations—both formal and informal—were not very impressive. I taught 5th and 6th graders, and it was clear that although the teachers in earlier grades had assigned front-of-the-class presentations from time to time, no one had given my students direct, specific instruction about how to present well.

I decided to teach these delivery skills, and began planning my instruction by examining exactly the kind of rubric-generated list of performance descriptors that we have just considered. Even though I liked many of the words on the list, there were too many of them for me to teach and for my students to master. My answer was *multiple-trait speaking* (Palmer, 2011), which boils the list down to six essential competencies:

- *Poise*—appearing calm and confident
- *Voice*—making every word heard
- *Life*—putting passion into the voice
- *Eye contact*—engaging each listener
- *Gestures*—matching motions to words
- *Speed*—pacing for a powerful performance

If you are familiar with multiple-trait writing, you know that efforts have been made to break writing into distinct components. Education Northwest (2013) champions 6+1 Trait® Writing, which advocates that all writing include *ideas, organization, word choice, sentence fluency, voice, conventions,* and *presentation*. Conceptualizing writing in this way provides shared vocabulary for both teachers and students and functions as both a scoring guide for evaluation and a tool to produce stronger writing. A student may have wonderful content but present it in a disorganized way. When she receives lower marks in the "organization" category, it's a cue to continue to work on improving in that area. The six traits apply at all grade levels, but the expectations can be scaled appropriately. In primary grades, "organization" means having a beginning, middle, and end. As students get older, the expectation expands to include proper use of transitions. Later, the organization expectation deepens. A 7th grade teacher, might, for example, teach students to replace a clunky or obvious beginning ("In this paper, I am going to tell you about climate change") with something more effective ("Our planet is heating up. In fact, it is dangerously overheating, and enormous problems will occur in your lifetime."). In other words, six-trait writing instruction allows teachers to develop specific lessons of varying complexity within the broad trait categories while retaining the simple and straightforward language.

I applied the same principles when I created multiple-trait speaking. The traits have the acronym "PVLEGS," and you will see that I refer to PVLEGS often.

Consider the trait *Voice*—making every word heard. We want students to know that every listener or viewer must be able to hear every word said. This expectation encompasses familiar and useful words and concepts from the big rubric lists, such as *volume, projection, loudly,* and *"speak up"*; it also includes less friendly, muddier words like *articulation, enunciation,* and *elocution.* If you teach early elementary school, you might first focus on teaching students to speak at an appropriate volume, as Standard 4 requires, and then teach them not to mumble, as mumbling prevents every word from being heard. If you teach higher grade levels, you can still talk about voice, but you might focus instruction on avoiding vocal tics, such as making every sentence sound like a question. The beauty of the PVLEGS approach is that the language remains consistent from class to class and grade to grade. The expectations shift, but the key concepts and basic framework do not.

Recall that Standard 4 is quite weak in discussing how to deliver a presentation. A student who masters PVLEGS will far exceed its minimal requirements. But also remember a comment I made some time ago: this book is not a Common Core Standards guide. While we need to address the standards, we need not be limited by them.

## ⊃ TAKE ACTION: Developing Delivery Skills

The strategies in this section all pertain to skills students need to speak well. The well-constructed message has no value unless it is also well spoken. I don't attempt to address all of the traits of effective performance here, but I do offer some simple techniques to begin the process of developing competent oral communicators.

### Expect more from students (K–12)

"But they are just kids. What do you expect?" "Aren't they adorable? They look so cute!" "Hey, not all kids are good at speaking.

That's just the way it is." "But this is authentic! They are using their authentic way of speaking." "I did give them some tips. You should've heard them *before!*"

I have heard all of these responses and more when I have suggested to teachers that the student I witnessed speaking was unimpressive. I realize that accepting criticism is difficult; we want to defend our students, and by extension, ourselves: (*How dare you pick on them (me!) and the way they talk?*) But we must be careful not to sell our students short.

Yes, they are young, and sometimes they are adorable, but they would be much better speakers with more guided instruction, based on multiple-trait speaking. Yes, some students are not as well spoken as others, just as some are not as facile with multiplication tables, reading, or drawing; still, all can be better oral communicators than they are. Yes, the way they speak may be authentic, but *competence* is not the opposite of *authentic*. Students can be *authentic and powerful speakers* or *authentic and mediocre speakers*. We don't do them any favors by making excuses for them or deemphasizing presentation skills.

Another common mistake many teachers make is enabling poor speakers:

> *Hannah* (speaking softly): I think we need to have a bake sale to raise money for our class pet.
>
> *Teacher:* Everyone, Hannah thinks we should have a bake sale. Do you agree?

If Hannah is speaking too softly, the better response would be this:

> *Hannah* (speaking softly): I think we need to have a bake sale to raise money for our class pet.
>
> *Teacher:* Hannah, *Voice.* I don't think everyone heard you.
>
> *Hannah:* I think we need to have a bake sale to raise money.
>
> *Teacher:* Better. Remember that *Voice* means "Every word heard." Did you all hear Hannah's idea now?

Similarly, we pay too much deference to the fear of speaking. Yes, some students are shy. How do we compensate for that? Imagine a student who struggles with multiplication tables. Do we say, "Timmy, I know that times tables are difficult for you, so every time there is a math problem that asks you to multiply two numbers, just look at me and I will give you the answer. Or you know what? Just don't do those and I will excuse all of them." No. We make accommodations—give Timmy more time, practice sessions at lunch or after school, and extra resources for practice. We don't feed into Timmy's math phobia. The idea is ridiculous.

As students are developing speaking competence and confidence, they may need extra encouragement, extra practice, and extra time before and during presentation performances. One of the best strategies to use is to let the student start over if things go poorly at first. Take the pressure off by acknowledging mistakes and creating a space for fixing them. But don't feel apologetic for helping them become better speakers.

### Use mini-speeches to practice key skills (K–12)

Typically presentations are fairly "high stakes" and almost always graded. What we don't do often enough is give small-scale oral assignments, complete with formative feedback, that are aimed at helping students develop specific performance skills.

Consider eye contact, for example. Every teacher knows that eye contact is a part of effective presentation, and the Common Core's Standard 4 requires students in 6th grade and above to use eye contact in their presentations. To teach this, try asking student volunteers to speak for up to one minute about a topic they love: favorite musical group, superhero, aunt or uncle, or place to go on vacation. At the end of these mini-speeches, call for the rest of the class to raise their hands if the speaker looked directly at them while talking. For speakers, this provides a vivid illustration of where they were looking and where they weren't (Palmer, 2011). Now, when eye contact is assessed during a big presentation, a student would be able to say, "I saw that I tend to look only at the middle of the room, so I made it a point to move my eye contact around the room. That's why I got a better grade this time."

Every aspect of multiple-trait speaking can be taught with similar practice activities. Along the way, students will have accomplished all of the performance components of Standard 4.

### Teach speaking across all curricula (K–12)

Jennifer is a high school teacher. In her graphic design class, she covers the technical tools and visual requirements of good design, and one of her assignments is for students to create a *glog*— a "graphic blog" or online interactive "poster" at Glogster (http://edu.glogster.com). Significantly, she doesn't stop there. Jennifer has students present their poster to the class, and she evaluates the presentation using the PVLEGS rubric. She teaches them the skills of presentation in the context of a graphic design lesson—a true life skill for graphic designers who will one day have to discuss their portfolios in front of hiring committees and specific work in front of design directors. Her assignment is shown in Figure 6.3.

### Use digital tools and sites for practice (4–12)

My smartphone has Easy Voice Recorder, a free application that records my voice for immediate playback or for attaching to an e-mail. The netbook I am using to write has Sound Recorder preinstalled for voice recordings. PCs have webcams and Macs have Photo Booth for simple video creation. Vocaroo (www.vocaroo.com) is a website for free voice recording. All of these give students a way to watch and listen to themselves as they present (Palmer, 2012). Think of how helpful rough drafts are for writing assignments; "rough drafts" of speaking assignments, with similar instructor and peer feedback, are similarly useful.

Try making a rough-draft recording of a presentation due about one week before students will be giving their final presentations. These rough drafts are ideally done as homework, with students having the option of using whatever tools are most convenient. Those who don't have access to the necessary technology might

**Figure 6.3** | A Graphic Design Presentation Assignment Evaluated with the Multi-Trait Speaking Rubric

## Unit of Study

Introduction

## Class Specifications

15 Freshman Mixed Schedule:
5 Period A, 10 Period A & B

## Preparation

Print worksheets for Making a Good Layout. Hand out Making a Good Layout workbook and have the students read it and fill out the corresponding worksheet. Post the samplings of good designs that the students printed from the Internet or found in print. Create a graphics glog with a favorite color, quote, song, and interactive links. Double-check the links to ensure the video, survey, and curriculum will appear when introducing the project to the freshmen.

## Presentation

Present the glog to the students as a sample and demonstration of expectations. Show them the video on Graphic Design, the link to the survey, and the GDVC Grade 9 Curriculum and expectation file. Review the specification of the glog to ensure a successful end product. Hand out this rubric, the PVLEGS rubric (attached) and the Schoolwide Speaking & Listening rubric (attached). Use the rubric to discuss the elements of a strong presentation.

## VTE Curriculum Frameworks

*Strand 2:* Technical Knowledge and Skills
*Strand 3:* Embedded Academic Knowledge and Skills
*Strand 4:* Employability Knowledge
*Strand 6:* Technological Knowledge and Skills
*(Specific strands for glog attached)*

## Project

"Glog Yourself" Presentation

## Objectives

- To create a project that introduces and expresses yourself to the class.
- To explore the industry you have chosen and share your interests with the class and instructor.
- To gain familiarity with the technical tools, ideas, and images related to the field of graphic design.

## Criteria

Your completed project for a grade should express yourself and must be saved to the Glogster website. Keep in mind you will be presenting your glog to the class and explaining the required specifications and how you included them in your glog.

(continued)

## Figure 6.3 — A Graphic Design Presentation Assignment Evaluated with the Multi-Trait Speaking Rubric—(continued)

**Sample Glog**

**Grade Level**

Freshman

**Programs**

www.google.com, www.youtube.com, edu.glogster.com

**Specifications**

Include the following in your glog:

*Personalization of Glog* (10 pts each)
Include things like favorite color, song, quote, photo, hobby.

*Definition of Type or Graphic Design* (15 pts)
Include a sample image with a definition or find a video that defines either one.

*Explanation of Choice Program* (10 pts)
Include a sample image with a definition or find a video that defines either Photoshop or InDesign.

*Presentation of Career Path* (10 pts)
Include a sample image with a definition or find a video that defines the college or job you wish to enter after high school.

*Element of Design Making a Statement* (10pts)
Using the workbook Good Layout, give a brief statement about the elements of design and how they are used to create a successful layout

*Sources Cited* (5 pts)
Include at least three sources used to build your glog.

**Grade**

| | |
|---|---|
| Personalization of Glog | 50% |
| Definition of Type or Graphic Design | 15% |
| Explanation of Choice Program | 10% |
| Presentation of Career Path | 10% |
| Element of Design Statement | 10% |
| Sources Cited | 5% |

*Source:* Jennifer Ayers, Plymouth South High School, Plymouth, Massachusetts. Used with permission.

take turns recording their presentations with school-owned tools in class or after school. The recordings might be submitted via e-mail or a URL.

I highly recommend having students view and provide input on their classmates' presentations, ideally using the same evaluation rubric you will be using for the final presentation. Peer editing works for writing; peer listening works for oral communication.

### Use digital tools and sites for showcasing speaking (K–12)

A science report with a trifold board is fast losing appeal to both student presenters and student audiences. Creating an online slideshow increases engagement in the learning task and also addresses technology standards. Utellstory (www.utellstory.com) is an online slideshow creation site that offers users the option to record voice narration. Students can create an image slide with pictures they upload, a video slide with YouTube or Vimeo videos, or a text slide. Then they can add their voice to each slide.

Yodio (www.yodio.com)—the name is a mash-up of "your" and "audio"—is a website that "makes audio publishing simple." After registering a phone number with the site, the user calls from a toll-free number from the registered phone and records a spoken presentation. Later, she can visit the site, access her recording, add images, and get a URL address to publish the recording.

Glance back at Standard 1 in Chapter 3. That standard is broken into subsections. The authors of the Common Core State Standards would have been wise to break Standard 4 into subsections as well—the two I've described, building the speech and performing the speech. When you talk with your class about the preparation needed *before speaking,* choose the language that works best for you and for them—*building the speech, crafting the message, creating the words, constructing the message,* or something similar. Make sure students know that what they do *while speaking* is an entirely different piece of oral communication, and it requires an entirely different set of skills. With that understanding and specific instruction, students can begin to develop the skills they need to be impressive in any speaking situation. When they can add powerful enhancements and learn how to adjust for their audience, they will be masterful communicators. We'll look at those subjects in the next chapters.

# 7

# INCORPORATING MULTIMEDIA

Chalkboards. Dry erase boards. Filmstrips. Opaque projectors. 16mm films. Overhead projectors. VHS machines hooked up to a TV. LCD projectors. Interactive whiteboards. I have seen teachers use all of these to present information to students. When I began consulting, I used flip charts and carried a giant pad of paper, an easel, and a set of very fat markers to every talk. That seems old-fashioned now, but it was not that long ago.

How have your own presentations evolved? What tools are you using now, and how long have you been using them? Who taught you how to use those tools? Would you be able to explain what makes a good PowerPoint slide or a good whiteboard visual? Do you know the most effective way to design a video tutorial, or how image and sound can be used to enhance learning?

When it comes to incorporating multimedia to make our instruction more powerful and promote understanding, most of us are just winging it. We have many new tools at our disposal, many of them digital, but our training has not kept up with the changes. We are using media without being particularly media literate, and now the

Common Core is asking us to teach students to do something that we haven't mastered ourselves.

## A Look at Standard 5

Standard 5 (SL.5) also falls under the "Presentation of Knowledge and Ideas" heading and focuses on incorporating multimedia into presentations—visual and audio components such as illustrations, graphics, video, and sound. The anchor standard articulates the goal, which is for students to graduate with the ability to **"make strategic use of digital media and visual displays of data to express information and enhance understanding of presentations."** Here is the grade-level progression of Standard 5:

> **Kindergarten:** Add drawings or other visual displays to descriptions as desired to provide additional detail.
>
> **Grade 1:** Add drawings or other visual displays to descriptions *when appropriate to clarify ideas, thoughts, and feelings.*
>
> **Grade 2:** *Create audio recordings of stories or poems;* add drawings or other visual displays to *stories or recounts of experiences* when appropriate to clarify ideas, thoughts, and feelings.

Nothing too unusual here. Teachers have always asked students to illustrate stories. But notice the purpose of the illustrations—to *clarify* something. Students are not asked to draw and then talk about the drawing but to talk and *then* add a drawing that complements the words they say. In addition, notice the technology requirement for grade 2. Now 2nd graders aren't just making traditional posters; they are making audio recordings to accompany their visual displays, which may or may not be posters.

> **Grade 3:** Create *engaging* audio recordings of stories or poems that demonstrate *fluid reading at an understandable pace;* add visual displays when appropriate to emphasize or *enhance certain facts or details.*
>
> **Grade 4:** Add audio recordings and visual displays to presentations when appropriate to enhance the development of main ideas or themes.

**Grade 5:** *Include multimedia components (e.g., graphics, sound)* and visual displays in presentations when appropriate to enhance the development of main ideas or themes.

There is an odd addition of a reading skill in the 3rd grade version of Standard 5. What I would really like to point out, though, is how the upper elementary standards increase the technology expectations. Yes, the focus is still on adding something to help develop main points, but that something must include high-tech enhancements. Third graders record themselves, but 4th and 5th graders must find and add audio to improve their messages. By 5th grade, poster board is gone. The standard expects graphics, sound, and, we might assume, video to be embedded in presentations.

**Grade 6:** Include multimedia components (e.g., graphics, images, music, sound) and visual displays in presentations *to clarify information.*

**Grade 7:** Include multimedia components and visual displays in presentations to clarify *claims and findings and emphasize salient points.*

**Grade 8:** *Integrate* multimedia and visual displays into presentations to clarify information, *strengthen claims and evidence, and add interest.*

Once again, we see the middle school shift to informational-only presentations. Students must clarify information, emphasize points, and strengthen evidence (though, in 8th grade, they are also allowed to focus on adding interest). Multimedia components are required. This is a significant shift from normal expectations for this age group; I doubt that many middle school book reports are currently embedded with soundtracks and images.

**Grades 9–12:** *Make strategic use of digital media (e.g., textual, graphical, audio, visual, and interactive elements)* in presentations *to enhance understanding of findings, reasoning, and evidence* and to add interest.

The addition of the word *strategic* seems to suggest a higher standard somehow. The reality is that high school students must continue to do what middle school students do—add multimedia components—and do it for the same reasons. Now we are asked to imagine a student speaking in front of the class with supporting text, graphs, images, and sounds. Students are almost compelled to use a computer to design and project the presentation. There is also the suggestion that talking at the class is not sufficient; there must be interactive elements.

Communication has changed. Video and image-based technologies have worked their way into our lives, and now, our classrooms. Knowing how to produce, edit, and share videos were not skills that many needed a generation ago, but increasingly these skills are in demand. Schools are using video on their websites to inform parents and share school activities. Teachers are creating online lessons. Students are producing videos at home, uploading them to YouTube, and sharing them with friends. It is increasingly difficult to find students with no access to digital media.

The challenge for educators is to show students how to effectively incorporate digital media to enhance their communication. This will be a stretch. Do *we* all effectively enhance *our* presentations and lessons with sound, image, and video? Do we know how to teach students that there is a difference between adding sound and adding sound that contributes to the point? Students are, for the most part, ahead of teachers in comfort with technology; it's probably wise to let them show us the tools. Our job will be to show them how to use the tools well.

## Understanding Presentation Literacy

Most classrooms teachers have various media options at their disposal, and these possibilities bring questions. Is a lesson better if it is presented on an interactive whiteboard? How do various media presentations affect learning? Should we embed a video? Use an online interactive game? What are the relevant merits of presenting a topic via a whiteboard and via a PowerPoint? How does either provide a better learning experience than a textbook? I'm not sure we, as teachers, have spent much time thinking about these questions, and I would guess that many of us aren't sure of the answers.

To our ever-expanding definition of literacy we must now add presentation literacy. I define it as having the skills and competencies to analyze, evaluate, and create presentations using a variety of tools and methods. These presentations may be designed for and delivered to a small audience or a large one; the audience can be in person or online. The presentations may use the poster board and trifold display boards that have long been common in schools, or they may use digital tools such as Glogster, LCD projectors and interactive whiteboards, and video or audio. Before we can help our students understand how these tools support communication and how to select the best tool for a particular purpose, we need to understand it ourselves.

## Selecting the medium

In communication, the medium matters. Imagine this situation: your family pet was hit by a car while your child was at school. How do you tell your child? Do you put a sticky note on the door for him to see when he comes home? Do you send him a text or an e-mail? Do you call? Set up a FaceTime call? Most of us would think that this kind of news requires a face-to-face conversation. Now imagine you're considering what visual components your elementary students might create to accompany presentations for the social studies unit "Colorado Trappers and Traders." Should you ask them to create shoebox dioramas? To create posters with bubble-letter labels, glued-on pictures, and word-processed text? To create an online, digital slideshow with embedded video and audio commentary? To create a Prezi—a cloud-based presentation enhanced with images that zoom in and out (see www.prezi.com)?

All these options exist. We have to help students be aware of the options—including "old school" ones, like simple, hand-drawn illustrations—and help them understand the reasons for choosing one over another. In other words, we have to look to *purpose*. Which medium best supports the presenter's purpose?

Continually ask students to justify their use of technology or media. A Prezi with slides zooming in from all different directions might be fun to watch, but does it suit a serious topic? Does it help us learn about poverty in America, or does it just make us think, "Wow, the way that spun in was cool"? Is a bulleted list of steps shown on a PowerPoint slide more effective than showing a video of the procedure? This kind of questioning must become common.

## Designing for the medium

How a presenter uses the medium matters as well. I speak at many conferences, which means I also spend a lot of time in the audience as others present. I absolutely understand "death by PowerPoint"—that numb, hopeless, and completely disinterested feeling you get when presenter after presenter after presenter projects PowerPoint slides that are poorly designed, overly complex, difficult to understand, visually ugly, or all of the above. One of the most famous examples of a dreadful slide came from the Office of the Joint Chiefs of Staff and was intended to show the path to achieving stability in Afghanistan. You can find it online by searching "terrible Afghanistan PowerPoint." General Stanley McChrystal, in charge of the war effort at the time, said, "When we understand that slide, we'll have won the war" (Bumiller, 2010, ¶2).

Few educators have received training in how to look critically at instructional media and how to teach students to create effective visuals for whatever media they are using. Adding to the problem are the features that are built in to the presentation tools most likely to be at our (and our students') disposal. PowerPoint and Keynote software offer many ways to easily ruin a slide, and interactive whiteboard software contains all sorts of useless, decorative, distracting elements to add to the screen. What should be simple and understandable becomes complex and confusing. Yes, one click will allow you to put smiley faces all over the screen, but should you do it? No. Never.

In his book *Multi-media Learning*, psychologist Richard E. Mayer (2009) examines the way words, pictures, and sounds can be combined to either support or hinder learning. Realizing that today's instructors are adding images and sounds to the verbal messages they have long relied on, he asks the following question: what presentations lead to *no learning*, to *rote learning* (characterized by good retention but not the ability to transfer the learning to other situations), and to *meaningful learning* (characterized by good retention *and* transference). Mayer conducted experiments to test the efficacy of every possible combination of sound, image, and narration, and the results are sometimes surprising. I want to highlight one key concept, the *limited capacity theory*.

Many educators believe that more media is better. If, while we are talking, we also give students a screen to look at with pictures and printed words and sometimes even sound effects, we'll be able to engage and reach different types of learners—visual, auditory, musical, logical, and so on. Intuitively, that seems reasonable.

Mayer offers a lot of evidence suggesting that this approach is wrong. He points out that learners are quickly overloaded. A student's auditory channel has a limited capacity. If she is listening to the teacher describe how thunder is created *and* hearing background music *and* hearing storm sounds, the auditory channel is overloaded. She cannot comprehend as much information as she could if the music and storm sounds were removed. Similarly, a student's visual channel has a limited capacity. If he is looking at a picture while trying to read the words at the bottom of the page, he will have problems. He has a better shot at meaningful learning if he is looking at a picture only (only one visual channel input) and listening to an explanation only (only one auditory channel input). Ironically, our attempts to reach all types of learners can make learning too difficult for all learners.

In addition to rethinking how much information we present on each slide or screen, we need to rethink how those slides or screens are structured. This is another area in which teachers get no instruction. No teacher preparation programs or in-service workshops I'm aware of focus on the proper design of classroom visuals. Indeed, our visuals often model poor design. We tend to "decorate" rather than design, adding extraneous items, distracting backgrounds, and unusual fonts. We think of these as adding visual interest, but if we are trying to "clarify ideas," "emphasize salient points," and "make strategic use of digital media" (as Standard 5 would have us teach students to do), this is counterproductive. What we should do instead is apply and model four key design principles: *simplicity, focus, color,* and *structure.*

**Simplicity.** Consistent with what we now know about limited capacity, slides and websites work best when they are streamlined. Author and popular speaker Garr Reynolds puts it this way:

> When I say we need to create messages and design visuals that are simple, I am not talking about taking shortcuts, or ignoring complexities, or endorsing meaningless sound bytes [sic] and shallow content. When I use the word simple (or simplicity), I am referring to the term as being essentially synonymous with clarity, directness, subtlety, essentialness, and minimalism. (2008, pp. 103–104)

Unfortunately, software developers have made it too easy to violate this principle. PowerPoint and Keynote have backgrounds that dominate the message. Whiteboard manufacturers have software that makes adding meaningless animations and images effortless. Resist these temptations and strive for clarity, directness, and essentialness. Ask the same kind of critical questions we asked about the choice of technology: why do you want that picture? Does it clarify something? Does it contribute to your words or take attention away from your words? Why that sound? Is it an annoying looping soundtrack found in the podcast creation software, or does it add to the mood you are trying to create? Following Mayer's and Reynolds's advice means teaching students to favor clean screens, few words, no "entertaining" animations, and no odd slide transitions. Style must not be permitted to detract from substance.

**Focus.** Too often presentation media make it difficult for the audience to figure out where to look first. Part of that problem can be addressed by simplification (removing the things we do not need to attend to); the rest can be addressed by designing better screen images (directing our eyes to the essential place). Look at Figure 7.1, which is a screenshot of an online tutorial on how to use GarageBand, a popular online application for creating music and podcasts.

| Figure 7.1 | An Unfocused Visual Presentation |
| --- | --- |

Do you see the GarageBand icon? Probably not. The very simplest part of using this application is to open it, and already the instructor is making that more difficult by getting in the audience's way. Viewers are drawn to the seascape that dominates the screen; the icon for launching the application is buried. Encourage students to get feedback before finalizing the presentation. "What is the first thing you notice here?" is an important question to ask.

**Color.** Yes, it is easy to change the color of the background and the color of the text. But ask whether changing the color is important. Does it add to the point? Then use it. Suddenly switching to red text may be a dramatic addition to the climate change presentation about rising temperatures, for example. Does it highlight something valuable? Convey important thoughts or feelings? Then use it. Also ask if the colors go well together. We have all seen presentations created with bright pink letters on a background of deep blue with yellow diagonal lines. Common, but ugly.

**Structure.** Think of this as "visual organization." Take a look at Figure 7.2. Which image would you say would be more effective in a presentation, A or B?

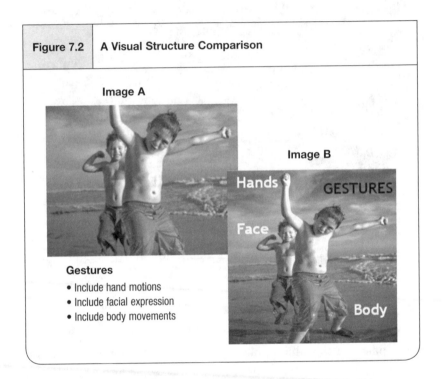

| Figure 7.2 | A Visual Structure Comparison |

**Image A**

**Image B**

Hands  GESTURES

Face

**Gestures**
- Include hand motions
- Include facial expression
- Include body movements

Body

Image A forces the viewer to look back and forth several times between the words beneath the photo and the photo at the top, juggling two visual inputs. Image B is structured so that the viewer has an easier time taking in the information. Each word is located close to the part of the image that is important for that word. Tell students to make things easy for the viewer. Fewer eye movements is the goal.

Simple changes in the way visuals are put together can increase their impact and promote learning. Of course, in addition to teaching students about these principles, we should use them ourselves to model Standard 5's requirement for strategic use of multimedia.

## ➲ TAKE ACTION: Developing Presentation Literacy

Let's look now at some strategies for helping students create better presentations.

### Discuss presentation types with students (K–12)

Even our youngest students are asked to use visual displays and audio to clarify information. That suggests that *all* students will benefit from discussion about what type of presentation best suits the information. Traditionally, teachers make this decision— "Make a tri-fold brochure" or "Make a poster" or "Use GarageBand to make an audio podcast." We need to challenge ourselves to justify our choices. For example, is a brochure the best way to introduce students to the South American country studied? Could the same content be presented more effectively with some other media? Couldn't an embedded video of native foods aid our understanding of Peru? These are essential questions to ask. Now, some more specific illustrations:

• *Grades K–5:* Show students pictures of the process of making bread, then read aloud a story about bread making, and then show a video of bread making inside a bakery. Ask students questions about the process. Require the students to mention the source with each answer. "What makes bread rise?" ("The video said that they add yeast.") "Did the story include the same information as the video? Which was more memorable? Which made it easier to understand how to make bread?" These types of discussions will guide students in selecting multimedia and visual displays to enhance main ideas.

• *Grades 6–8:* Find multiple media sources pertaining to a topic—say, cell division. Find a video, a PowerPoint, a poster, and an audio description of the process. Ask students about the types of media. "Which version did you prefer? Why? What worked better in the PowerPoint than in the video?" ("It was slower and I had more time to get the picture.") "What worked better in the video than in the audio?" ("I needed to see it to get it.") "How did the poster help clarify the text? Did the music playing during the audio narration contribute to your understanding?"

- *Grades 9–12:* Continue the type of questioning shown in the middle school example. To go beyond that level of discussion, show the video "Life After Death by PowerPoint" (McMillan, 2010). Discuss the key points of the presentation captured in the video. Then ask, "How did that PowerPoint change the way you might design your presentations?" Next, discuss McMillan's presentation as a presentation. How did *he* present? Was *his method* successful? Challenge students to find their own examples of presentations in different media that worked well and have them explain what elements of the presentation supported their understanding or made it more interesting.

After these discussions, ask students to create a presentation. If you usually have students do a research project and present to the class, ask them to design their talk with the discussion in mind. Require them to explain what they added and why.

### Create a bank of "media awareness" questions (6–12)

In Chapter 5 we created question starters for discussions in general. Now work with students to generate question starters for media awareness. Here are some examples:

- "How did the images make you feel about...?"
- "How did the music make you feel?"
- "Did the lighting contribute to the overall feeling of...?"
- "Why were the shots constructed the way they were?"
- "What did the editing/montage do for the effect of...?"
- "Did the images used help convey the message?"
- "Did the interaction at the whiteboard add or detract from the learning?"
- "Did the slides seem too complex? Too simple?"
- "Did the design of the visual aids work for you? Did they add or detract?"

Again, after the discussions, require students to write about their own presentation. "Well, based on our talk about montage, I slowed down the edited images in my video because I wanted each image to sink in a bit" or "I sped up the editing to create a feeling of excitement."

### Provide or create tools for video analysis (6–12)

In Chapter 4, I introduced a photo analysis worksheet created by the education department of the National Archives. The same team created a worksheet to guide the analysis of motion pictures. Available at www.archives.gov/education/lessons/worksheets, it calls students' attention to the physical aspects of movie or video (including music, narration, special effects, and so on) and prompts them to think about how these aspects contribute to the piece's tone. It's a great tool for helping students identify and understand the messages in videos they watch. I also recommend modifying the National Archives' original form to be a tool for video production. By turning some of the questions around, as in Figure 7.3, you've got a tool for *designing* video that coordinates very nicely with the scaffolding in Standard 5.

### Create PechaKucha and Ignite presentations (Grades 8–12)

The PechaKucha presentation format was created in Tokyo in 2003 as a way to streamline presentation design and delivery (Reynolds, 2008.) A PechaKucha presentation consists of exactly 20 slides, each displayed for exactly 20 seconds. The slides advance automatically, and when they are done, the presenter is done. There are no follow-up comments, no "Let me add just a couple more things before we move on." Twenty slides, 20 seconds each, done.

Some argue that this kind of fast-paced presentation contributes to the limiting of attention spans and the rewiring of brains so that we can no longer listen to complex messages or focus for sustained periods of time. It's true that PechaKucha is designed to avoid

| Figure 7.3 | A Tool for Creating Video Presentations |
| --- | --- |

**Title Meaning**

What title will you use?

What are three concepts or ideas you want people to think about when they hear the title?

**Purpose**

What is the intent of the video? (Check all that apply.)
☐ To instruct
☐ To persuade
☐ To entertain
☐ To ask for action
☐ To demonstrate a procedure
☐ Other

What is your core message? Write only one good sentence.

What techniques/features will add to the desired effect? (Check all that apply and describe).
☐ Lighting:
☐ Music type/song titles:
☐ Camera angle:
☐ Animation:
☐ Titles:
☐ Sound effects:
☐ Costumes:
☐ Diagrams:
☐ Editing/montage:
☐ Other:

details, and it moves too quickly for deep thought. However, supporters of the format would point out that details and deep thought are intended to come after the presentation, as audience members discuss what they have seen or go off on their own, motivated to learn more about the topic.

Ignite (tagline: "Enlighten us, but make it quick") is an organization that sponsors events in which speakers talk about personal issues and professional passions in presentations restricted to 20 slides that automatically advance every 15 seconds. Every presentation comes in at a tidy five minutes, which is about the length of a typical classroom presentation. Visit the website page (www.ignite show.com) and show students examples of how much information can be communicated in just five minutes.

Focusing on the PechaKucha and Ignite format guidelines and asking students to adhere to them is a way to underscore the importance of using media carefully and thoughtfully. Summarization is essential, as is being concise and choosing words well.

## Focus on avoiding listener/viewer overload (4–12)

Mayer (2009) believes the key to reducing extraneous processing overload is to follow five principles of presentation: *coherence, signaling, redundancy, spatial contiguity,* and *temporal contiguity.* Although we may not want to use this exact language when introducing the ideas to our students, this advice is sound and should be shared. It boils down to this:

• *Eliminate unnecessary words, sounds, or pictures.* The cute graphic of the snowman on the bottom of the screen (because winter break is approaching) and the repetitive music looping detract from learning how to find the least common multiple.

• *Highlight.* Point out key words and important parts of the graphics.

• *Don't ask the audience to read the words you are saying.* Get rid of picture captions if you are verbally explaining the visual.

• *Put key words right next to the image.* Don't have a bank of words on the side. Instead, put the labels right on the picture.

• *Synchronize pictures and explanations.* Don't show a picture and then describe it; don't tell about something and then show the picture. The words and the media go together.

## Teach design principles and include them in assessments (4–12)

Cover the differences between decorating and designing, basing this instruction on the four principles of design we've discussed: simplicity, focus, color, and structure. Lead group critiques of all kinds of presentations—everything from the old-school "book report cubes" (the main character on one side, climax on one side, and so on) and trifold "vacation brochures" capturing data on various geographic regions or countries to the new-school examples you create using Notebook software for SMART Boards, ActivInspire software for Promethean interactive whiteboards, and instructional videos posted on YouTube or TeacherTube. Evaluate all for the same characteristics—simplicity, focus, color, and structure—and hold them all to the same standard.

## Teach selection bias (8–12)

The documentary filmmaker Morgan Spurlock became famous after his movie *Supersize Me* captured his experiment of eating McDonald's food for every meal, every day, for 30 days. He went on to apply the same approach in a television series called *30 Days*, in which people do a thing for one month, including working as a coal miner, living on minimum wage, and living as an illegal immigrant. I use that last example with students as a way to understand how editorial choices reveal bias. The episode "Immigration" describes the 30 days that Frank, a member of a volunteer border patrol group, lives in a one-bedroom apartment in with the Gonzalezes, a family of illegal immigrants. Frank is impressed with how hard the father works under conditions that are quite difficult; impressed with the daughter, an excellent student and an excellent golfer; and impressed with the family's cohesiveness and spirit. At one point in the show, Frank accompanies the Gonzalezes on a trip back to their Mexican hometown, which is a grim and poverty-stricken place.

At the end of his 30 days, Frank is much more sympathetic to the motives and plight of illegal immigrants than he originally was.

Understanding of selection bias prompts us to ask why Spurlock choose the Gonzalez family as representative of undocumented workers in America instead of any other family he could have chosen. Were they the "most typical"? What evidence would support or discredit that claim? And by choosing to send Frank to live with Gonzalezes rather than another family—perhaps a family that was not such a model of hard work and good habits and clean living—how were Spurlock and his producers shaping a particular message? Use this show as an example of how a presenter can select information to fit a particular point of view. The information doesn't need to be false; it's not lying. But which stories we choose to tell can make a difference, and selecting the story that fits a certain purpose is a common way of manipulating viewers.

After sharing this information with students, have them create movies about your school. Break them into two groups. The goal of the students in Group A is to capture the school looking terrible; Group B will work to capture the school looking great. Review the ways in which they can communicate certain messages: camera angles and lighting; choice of images (e.g., use footage of a student yawning or footage of students laughing? Of an empty hallway with an abandoned paper blowing down it or a busy, engaged classroom?). It will become clear that on the same day at the same school, two very different perspectives could be "correct."

### Teach the power of music and images (3–12)

Standard 5 gets students started incorporating musical and visual elements into presentations in early elementary school; they need guidance on how to do so purposefully and thoughtfully. I talked earlier about how software developers have made it easy to add meaningless graphics and animated images to our presentations. Podcast software such as GarageBand makes it easy to add meaningless sound, as well. Presenters can choose from a bank of prerecorded music options and then loop the recording so that it incessantly repeats. The intent is to provide a soundtrack just like they have in the movies, I suppose, but most often, the effect is a distraction. Music creates moods. Actor and comedian Steve Martin joked that no one could be unhappy listening to banjo music. Conversely, few people are moved to laughter by Mozart's *Requiem*.

Teach students to select music that adds to the message and is consistent with the mood they are trying to create. Video some audio-free student presentations. Create an audio recording of several different genres of music, looping sound tracks, and sound effects. Play a video several times with different background music each time. Ask the students: "Did any of these soundtracks help? Did they distract? What sounds would emphasize this speaker's message?" Require students to add some audio to the next presentation, and ask them to explain why they made the addition.

When it comes to focusing on how images work to communicate, emphasize, clarify, or enhance facts, details, ideas, and themes, news media provide solid teaching tools. What ideas do we get about the war in Afghanistan if we see a soldier smiling at Afghan children on the street? What ideas do we get about that war if we see a soldier in a firefight with wounded bodies near him? Select some images (or assign students the job of searching Google Images, for instance) for competing images: a picture of the president that makes him look great versus one that makes him look foolish or mean; a picture of New York that makes the city look like a place to visit versus a picture of New York that makes the city look like a place to avoid; and so on. Challenge students to explain their thinking: "Why does this make New York look inviting?" "Why might someone print this picture instead of that one?" Require students to explain the purpose behind each image they include in their presentation.

### Use 21st century tools (2–12)

By the end of elementary school, students need to be adept at adding digital media to presentations. Many tools are readily available, but I'll highlight a few here.

First, remember that many computers have webcams built in, and most digital cameras can capture both video and still pictures.

Students might use inexpensive cameras with built-in USB capability to create and edit video, and they can use smartphones to capture images and video. Encourage students to use these tools to create enhancements for their presentations.

Online sites are good options for activities that will help students build these skills. Meograph (www.meograph.com) is an easy-to-navigate site where students can "create, watch, and share interactive stories" by uploading images and video and then adding narration. The end product can be shared on the class or school web page, e-mailed to interested parties, or simply shown in class. Meograph also works very well in a UDL-focused classroom, allowing students the option to record and play a "performed" presentation rather than delivering it live. And because the audience is potentially much larger than the 30 classmates, creating a Meograph presentation may generate more interest and effort than the traditional report.

Narrable (www.narrable.com), a website that lets students give voice to pictures, is another I recommend. Students can upload images and record narration directly or have someone call in to talk about the image. For example, Narrable can transform a traditional "make a family tree" assignment into a creative, collaborative, digital presentation. After a student uploads family images, family members can call in to talk about those images. As viewers look at the picture of a student's grandfather, they hear his grandfather's voice describing life when he was a boy or his experience coming to America.

## Teach advanced media skills (9–12)

Most audio and video production software have a basic podcast-in-a-minute/video-in-a-minute capability, and most computers and tablets have either that functionality built in or can access it. There are even podcast-creating and movie-making phone apps (Videolicious for the iPhone, for example) that are transforming what were once rare skills into something doable for many. The basics of these programs can be mastered by younger students, while older students can move beyond the basics. Ducking an audio track so it does not dominate, bringing the sound volume up at certain points, adding a sound effects track in addition to the voice and music tracks, and more are possible with most applications. Editing, enhancing, and altering video clips and images can be easily done with programs readily available. These tools are keys to adding interest to digital presentations and to getting students to use digital media strategically. While we may not be able to teach the ins and outs of the programs, we can use the expertise in the room. Some students in upper grades are creating all the time and have lots to offer their classmates. Once you review key concepts and components (the importance of sound, sound level, montage), step to the side and let a student expert lead the learning on how to incorporate these into presentations.

Standard 5 draws upon the lessons of Standard 2. Students become critical receivers of information and then become critical presenters of information. The overriding theme of this book is to make our teaching of listening and speaking more purposeful. Both are part of every class already, but both can be more specifically addressed.

The way forward is to add new requirements to the presentations that you already ask students to do. Maybe you can ask them to include one song and one image to their "What I Did This Summer" talk. Maybe you can ask them to provide supplemental explanation: a paragraph explaining why they chose to present in Prezi rather than PowerPoint.

The age of simply talking is gone. Audiences today expect more. And speaking of audiences, let's move on to how to tailor presentations for them.

# 8

# ADAPTING FOR THE OCCASION

"I ain't mad atcha" or "I am not angry with you." Which should you say?

Well, we're teachers. Our quick response: "The latter."

Grammar and usage are typical components of speech rubrics—topics students need to think about as part of building a spoken presentation. But that doesn't mean it's always correct to choose "proper" grammatical constructions. The correct response to the question above is actually to ask another question altogether: "Who is the audience?"

Wisely, the Common Core standards recognize that speaking is much more than public speaking in a formal presentation. We speak in many contexts and to many different audiences—different sizes, different ages, different backgrounds, different media. No one style of speaking fits all of the situations in which we will find ourselves.

## A Look at Standard 6

As noted, Standard 6 (SL.6), the last under the "Presentation of Knowledge and Ideas" heading, is all about speaking and the language we choose when speaking. The ultimate aim is to produce high school graduates who can "adapt speech to a variety of contexts and communicative tasks, demonstrating command of formal English when indicated or appropriate." Let's look at the grade-level progression.

**Kindergarten:** *Speak audibly and express thoughts, feelings, and ideas clearly.*

**Grade 1:** *Produce complete sentences when appropriate to task and situation.*

**Grade 2:** Produce complete sentences when appropriate to task and situation *in order to provide requested detail or clarification.*

In the primary grades, the objective is to let students know that sometimes a complete sentence is expected (and, therefore, sometimes it is *not* expected). This is the beginning of understanding that speech must be adapted to the situation. It is left to teachers to determine "appropriate" situations. For example, when a student answers a question with a one-word response like "Because," it makes sense to ask the student to expand that response. ("We have to give dogs water because dogs get thirsty.")

**Grade 3:** *Speak in* complete sentences when appropriate to task and situation in order to provide requested detail or clarification.

**Grade 4:** *Differentiate between contexts that call for formal English (e.g., presenting ideas) and situations where informal discourse is appropriate (e.g., small-group discussion); use formal English when appropriate to task and situation.*

**Grade 5:** *Adapt speech to a variety of contexts and tasks,* using formal English when appropriate to task and situation.

In upper elementary, students are expected to realize that different situations call for different speaking styles. Teachers need to introduce the concept of "formal English" and make students aware of when it is required. Contrary to the assertion in the 4th grade version of the standard, formal English is *not* always needed for presenting ideas. It is not the genre of the talk but the makeup of the audience that should guide language choices. I'll say more about this a little later.

> **Grades 6–12:** Adapt speech to a variety of contexts and tasks, *demonstrating command* of formal English *when indicated* or appropriate.

Although the wording of Standard 6 changes a bit from kindergarten through 5th grade, the expectations do not. Neither the wording nor the expectations change at all throughout middle and high school. Students must recognize when to change communicative styles. There is the suggestion that the variety of contexts and tasks demands only one adaptation choice: use formal English or not?

From an instructional standpoint, is not difficult to get the concept of Standard 6 across. From very young ages, students realize that they speak differently at recess than they do when presenting book reports, and differently in the locker room than in front of Grandma. Our goal, though, is to make this intuitive adjustment purposeful and to make students aware of it as a skill to be developed and used.

## Understanding Formal English

In 2010, Senator Harry Reid got in some trouble for commenting about President Obama's lack of a "negro dialect," which the president seemed to use sometimes but not at all times. The president responded this way:

> I think there's a certain black idiom that it's hard not to slip into when you're talking to a black audience because of the audience response. It's the classic call and response. You know, anybody who has spent time in a black church knows what I mean, and so, you know, you get a little looser. It becomes more—a little more like jazz and a little less like a set score. (National Public Radio, 2010, ¶14)

The comments led to a broader recognition of "code switching." I use the phrase to mean specifically switching between dialects or styles of speech. Marc Lamont Hill, a professor of education and

African-American studies at Columbia University, explains that code switching is a way "to provide some kind of either social distance or social proximity to the people with whom you're speaking" (National Public Radio, 2010, ¶16). In this case, the discussion was about switching from, in Reid's poorly chosen words, "negro dialect" to what might be called standard English or, in the language of Standard 6, "formal English." Code switching extends beyond racial or ethnic speech, of course; I have heard teachers using language at a Friday afternoon happy hour that I have never heard them use in class.

To be successful speakers, we all need to code switch. The key point is that applying "right/wrong" labels to differing styles of speech is inappropriate. As Hill points out, African-American English is a thoughtful, systematic, and, he might have added, effective way to communicate. "Right/wrong" depends on the audience. It would be foolish to use a dialect that distances you from your audience, and it would be foolish not to use a dialect that brings you closer to your audience. Recall the question at the start of this chapter. What if "I ain't mad atcha" is common and acceptable in the community? Using that phrase would make a speaker more successful with that audience. Adjusting language is a way to connect with the audience, and connecting with the audience is the goal of all oral communication (Palmer, 2011). And those adjustments involve much more than sometimes switching to formal English, as Standard 6 suggests.

We do have to let students know that occasionally they will be asked to use formal English. But be careful. The word "formal" has some connotations that can mislead students. It suggests using archaic words, big words, and odd phrases in an attempt to be fancy. "Let's use the camera to make a video" becomes "At this point in time, we should utilize the camcorder in order to produce a video recording." Formal also implies a dress code and a stiff manner of delivery. For these reasons, I suggest avoiding the term altogether. I prefer to use language introduced by Lisa Delpit (2006) in her book *Other People's Children*. She writes about the need to "communicate effectively in standard, generally acceptable literary forms" and says students "must be taught the codes needed to participate fully in the mainstream" (pp. 18–19). Her way of thinking about communication rules is broader yet much more accurate than "formal" and "informal":

> There are codes and rules for participating in power; that is, there is a "culture of power." The codes and rules I'm speaking of relate to linguistic forms, communicative strategies, and presentation of self; that is, ways of talking, ways of writing, ways of dressing, ways of interacting. (p. 25)

Mainstream rules for communication exist, and those who wish to participate in the culture of power must use the rules of that culture. To teach students to look for the culture of power and adapt their speech to it is an invaluable life skill. What's more, in our wired and connected world, what is an acceptable way of speaking in Los Angeles may not be acceptable in New York; what works in New York may not work in London; and what works in London may not work in Bangalore or Riyadh. If students learn to understand the acceptable forms of the culture of power of the target audience, they will be successful. Sometimes that means we say, "I am not angry with you."

## Understanding Audience

Standard 6 uses the word *context*. "What is the context?" is primarily asking "To whom are you speaking?" Speakers adapt for their audience. Yes, we will make some adjustments if we are talking to one person (small voice) or to students in the bleachers (big voice), but students don't have a hard time understanding that part of context—the physical situation. The most important part of all oral communication is adapting to the people situation: a one-on-one discussion? A small-group situation? A large-group situation? In person or digital?

It amazes me how often speakers miss this point and fail to analyze their audience. Remember the afternoon faculty meeting about RTI that I referred to in Chapter 4? The person from the staff development office came in with the same presentation she always used, but this time, her audience was tired, restless, even a little resentful. She failed to ask the key question: "Is this approach going to work with this audience at this time?"

No doubt you too have been to talks where the speaker didn't understand the audience. Maybe he told you things you already knew or used incomprehensible insider jargon. Maybe he delivered a too-casual speech at a formal or solemn affair or a stuffy and didactic presentation when everyone else was ready to have a good time. If adults can be so inept at designing a speech for a specific group, it's no wonder children struggle with this task. They need instruction on how to talk in front of various audiences, and that's what Standard 6 can help teachers deliver.

Here is something I heard during a 7th grader's health class presentation:

> *Student:* Saturated fat can raise total blood cholesterol levels and low-density lipoprotein cholesterol levels, too. This may cause cardiovascular disease.

I can't challenge the accuracy of the statement, because that is exactly what the source material says. However, I *can* challenge the appropriateness of the statement for the listeners. Most 7th graders are probably not familiar with "lipoprotein cholesterol" (although if all students are researching health issues, the listeners in that situation may be somewhat familiar with cholesterol), and there are probably few 7th graders who understand cardiovascular disease. What we have here is an example of a student presenting information without any consideration of the audience. It happens all the time in our classrooms.

Here is the background for the situation I've just described: the teacher gave each student a health topic to research; she gave them a date for an oral presentation; she required certain content (e.g., the name of the nutrient/food, importance to the body, proper amounts); and she gave them a score sheet that would be used to evaluate the presentation, featuring aspects of performance like eye contact, attention to time limit, and posture. In this case, the student got maximum marks by accomplishing what was asked. Unfortunately, the class got nothing from the presentation, leading us to ask another important question: "Who are student presenta-tions really for?"

Although the teacher is part of the audience and may under-stand the content, the *real* audience, as far as the student presenter is concerned, is the rest of the class—his or her peers. It's a fairly easy audience for the presenter to analyze and, thus, a good place to start in terms of instruction and practice. The trickier job is to help students design a speech for a different audience, especially if the audience is unfamiliar, very diverse, or from a community radically different than the community students know.

The way to prepare students to adapt to different audiences and speaking contexts is to provide meaningful practice with a range of different audiences and contexts. Fortunately, our wired and con-nected world offers many ways to do this. Preparing and delivering a talk for a podcast, a video presentation, or a Skype presentation forces students to analyze the audience and adjust appropriately. Take advantage of these tools. A web search will reveal a large num-ber of educators who want to link up digitally. For example, at ePals Global Community (www.epals.com), you can select partner classes by age, region, and topic. A less-exotic option could simply be ask-ing your students to create a video presentation for the elderly resi-dents of an assisted living facility.

## ➲ TAKE ACTION: Developing Students' Ability to Adjust for Audiences

All of the strategies I suggest in this section are about guiding stu-dents to consciously adapt speech to the context and audience. The distinction between context and task will become obvious as you continue reading this chapter. First, we will look at how a speaking task (e.g., provide information) can be designed differently based on the context (e.g., an in-class presentation with parents in the audi-ence or a podcast for the class web page). It's true that there are cases in which the context (e.g., the locker room just before the big game) definitely drives the task, but here, we will focus on adapting the task for the situation.

## Teach students to be audience-aware (K–12)

Whenever an assignment is given that involves talking to an audience (this includes mock interviews, discussions, book chats, digital stories, and podcasts), begin with an explicit caution to students to think about the audience and design the talk for them (Palmer, 2011, 2012). Here are some practice scenarios to throw out and discuss:

• You are passionate about a kind of music but not all of your classmates like it. How can you interest all of us as you talk about this?

• We will have an in-class discussion about whether or not we should end art classes in our school. Come prepared to state your opinion and defend your position on the issue. Think about what arguments will be persuasive to class members.

• You researched your topic and know a lot about it. We didn't research it, and our class may not know many of the terms you are now familiar with. How can you explain to our age group the important things we need to know?

For any of these scenarios, ask students to answer the following questions:

1. Who is going to be in the audience?
2. What do they already know about the topic?
3. What do they need to know about the topic?
4. What mood are they in?
5. What are they expecting?
6. How will they be experiencing the presentation—in person, on a small tablet screen, projected on a large screen, some other way?
7. What content adjustments need to be made to suit this audience?
8. How should visuals be constructed to meet the audience's needs?
9. What kind of language will match the language of the audience?

## Use digital technology to provide practice addressing different audiences (K–12)

The idea that students need practice to improve is widely accepted in just about every area of instruction except listening and speaking. As I mentioned, with 21st century tools, it is easy to change the audience. Examples are everywhere.

Students at Tiverton Middle School in Rhode Island can participate in a Meet the Author Book Club. They read one book a month and then Skype that book's author (Gagne, 2012). Skype (www. skype.com) is free to use, making it possible to bring authors and experts into the classroom digitally. In this case, students learn about the writing process from the point of view of a person who makes a living writing, and they get to consider how they should adjust their language when asking questions of this professional adult. Is digital communication "less formal" than face-to-face conversation? While the point of Tiverton's club is to encourage writing, it would be a mistake to allow students to sit slouched in chairs, twirling the strings of their hoodies, while asking, "Um, you know how you like made the character like kinda not follow the rules and stuff? Was that like based on you or something?"

Many teachers are creating videos and posting them on YouTube. This provides an excellent way to change the audience. In some cases, the message may be intended for people of different ages and in different communities. What adaptations are needed to appeal to a broad audience? What language will have the widest acceptance?

## Understanding Different Types of Speeches

Just as we can prepare students for different speaking contexts by asking them to analyze the intended audience, we can prepare them for different speaking tasks by asking them to prepare multiple kinds of presentations. Recall my experience with book reports when I began teaching. I was told to assign an oral book report per quarter. The first quarter, I assigned a mystery book; the second quarter, a biography; the third quarter, a piece of historical fiction; and the fourth quarter, a piece of animal realism. Although I thought I was assigning four different speeches, I was basically assigning the same speech four times. Many teachers make the same mistake and limit the kind of speaking they ask students to do.

Most speeches fall into four categories—or *tasks,* to stick with the language of Standard 6. Let's look at these closely:

• *Informative*—a speech designed to provide information to the audience. Examples include a teacher lecturing about the religions of China, my students talking about the books they had read, and a businessperson explaining a new product to the sales staff.

• *Persuasive*—a speech designed to convince listeners to believe or do something. Examples include a student trying to convince the rest of the health class to eat fewer sugary snacks, a co-worker attempting to get us to donate blood, or a candidate urging us to vote for her.

• *Entertaining*—a speech designed to amuse and provide laughter. Examples include a student retelling a humorous happening on the field trip or a comedian poking fun at a famous celebrity.

• *Demonstrative*—a "how-to" speech. It is informative in a sense but also has a practical application. Examples would be a ski instructor teaching beginners how to snowplow to a stop, a tech specialist showing a teacher how to add questions to a whiteboard lesson, or a teacher showing students how to fill out the forms for the school magazine sale.

Yes, most of what is assigned in schools are informative speeches—book reports and lab reports and talks on the economics of a country, a historical figure, or a topic in the news. Demonstrative speeches occasionally make an appearance: "How to Solve the Equation" or "How to Dissect the Eyeball," for instance. Persuasive and entertaining speeches may be covered in schools with a dedicated speech class, but few other teachers ever assign them; there just isn't time.

The division between the speech types is not as clear as the definitions suggest. Certainly, I can relay lots of information in a speech intended to persuade you to, say, reduce the amount of fat calories in your diet. *The Daily Show* is on the Comedy Central network, but host Jon Stewart imparts a lot of information about current events (albeit with a liberal slant) as he goes about his real purpose: making his audience laugh. To teachers concerned that there is no time for anything that doesn't contribute to content coverage, I would say that it is possible to cover content *and* assign more than informative or demonstrative speeches. It just takes planning.

## ➲ TAKE ACTION: Developing Students' Sense of Task

These strategies will help students craft messages for particular purposes. They give students practice adapting to the task.

### Assign different speech situations (K–12)

Consider a teacher who is committed to developing students' oral language skill. She has students give book reports, talk about the best thing they did over the weekend, give a persuasive speech about a topic of their choice, dress up as a historical figure and present an eyewitness account of a famous event. She even has them deliver a "monologue" book report, in which they speak from the perspective of a book's central character, explaining their thoughts, feelings, and impressions on what happened. She's giving her students practice with various kinds of speech situations, right? Wrong. This is one speech format, replayed over and over again: one student in front of the class, talking for three to five minutes.

Let's look first at what this teacher is doing that's good: assigning different speech categories (informational, persuasive) and addressing a variety of topics. She's mirroring the Common Core's emphasis on informational speaking that incorporates details, evidence, descriptions, facts, and examples. She's also incorporating the standards' undervalued focus on recounting events and storytelling. The variety she is offering her students within the five-minute, stand-and-deliver speech is great. But all of these are still five-minute, stand-and-deliver speeches.

What this teacher—and all teachers—must remember to do is vary speech situations. That means structured speaking opportunities and unstructured ones. For starters, offer many more opportunities to get up in front of the class in low-stakes, short speeches. These give students a chance to practice the skills we will be looking for in later, higher-stakes speeches, and they are critical to developing speaking confidence (Palmer, 2011). We tend to value, critique, and score speaking only a couple of times a year. To truly help students, we need to be clear that we are concerned about oral communication *every time students talk in front of an audience*—even if the audience is three peers in the same breakout group, and even if they are informally discussing a solution to a problem or offering a comment in class. The Standard 6 speaking requirements should be part of our everyday expectations.

Try altering the format for some of the high-stakes speeches, too. For example, replace the individual book report with a team book report. After five children have all finished the same book, ask them to collaborate to present a talk show, in which one student (the host) interviews the other characters from the book. The host has to prepare excellent questions: "Huck, can you explain what you were thinking when…?" "Jim, do you feel bad about…?" The students must be well versed in the novel to respond in the way that their character would.

There is another benefit here, as well. As characters adopt a talk show participant persona, they modify the character persona found in the story. You can discuss the difference between how characters would talk in the TV studio versus in the book. In the upper grades, try having the characters interviewed by different people in different contexts. A character interviewed by "an elementary school librarian" should speak differently than when interviewed by "an entertainment reporter for the local news." Code switching might be required, depending on the locale of that news program.

Another strategy is to let two students present as one. I used to have "The World's Greatest Expert" come to my class. I selected two students to sit in chairs at the front of the room and explained that they were to think of themselves as one person, and that together they were the foremost authority on the topic we were studying. At my signal, a student asked the "expert" a question, and one of the two chosen students began the answer. At some point mid-sentence, I would clap my hands, and the other student had to begin speaking right where the first student had been cut off:

*Class member:* Expert, how can we adapt for the drought?

*Expert A:* First, we have to begin to conserve water. We need to take shorter showers, water our—

[CLAP]

*Expert B:* —um, lawns less, and don't let faucets drip.

*Class member:* Why is there a drought?

*Expert B:* No one is totally sure. Some people say climate change is affecting weather patterns. The high winds in the upper atmosphere do not blow the same—

[CLAP]

*Expert A:* —the same way they used to, so they don't blow the clouds the same way. Maybe it is just bad luck. Over history, sometimes there are dry periods.

This activity is clearly an exercise in careful listening, and it's an engaging and involving way for students to present information to one another. Use it occasionally for fun and silliness, too:

*Teacher:* Class, here is The World's Greatest Expert on peanut butter. Any questions?

*Class member:* Which is better, crunchy or creamy?

*Expert A:* Creamy, because what you don't know is that the crunch is really made up of ground-up bones of the mice that they—

[CLAP]

*Expert B:* —they capture around the factory. But mice bones aren't bad for you, so don't worry.

*Class member:* What is your favorite way to eat peanut butter?

*Expert B:* Well, I like to spread it on meat loaf and put M&Ms on top. The M&Ms really add—

[CLAP]

*Expert A:* —really add the crunch that I miss, because it is creamy peanut butter.

This activity makes clear that even in informal discourse, we can value and develop speaking skills.

## Role play (K–12)

Role-playing activities are a great way for students to practice adapting their speaking to task and context. I worked with students enrolled in the Advancement Via Individual Determination (AVID) program at Overland High School in Aurora, Colorado. Some students were competing for college scholarships offered by a charitable institution in Denver. We researched to learn about the type of people who were likely to be on the scholarship fund committee. We set up practice interviews, with some students acting as scholarship candidates and others as members of the interview panel. Both candidates and panel members adapted their speech accordingly, and playing these parts provided a great lesson in adjusting to the task.

In the primary grades, role-playing might be more heavily weighted toward the "play," with one student acting the part of a wise grandparent as other students ask for advice. How would a grandparent talk? What changes do we make when we are addressing a grandparent instead of, say, a fellow student? In upper elementary and beyond, offer some roles that require formal English (e.g., the talk show host) and some that don't (e.g., a sports reporter interviewing the Skateboard Vert gold medalist at the X Games).

Intuitively, we all know that it's natural to adapt speech to the circumstances. The temptation is to say, as we have said about many listening and speaking skills, "Students already do this. We don't have to teach it." But being able do something without thinking is not the same as purposefully developing the implicit core skill. All students benefit when we specifically teach these core skills and provide guided practice. They can get better at adapting their speech to a variety of contexts and tasks only if we make that part of our instruction.

As with the previous five Common Core standards, all instruction we offer to address this standard will improve our students' lives well beyond their school years. But how will we know if we are on the right track? How can we assess students' progress? We'll look at that next.

# 9

## ASSESSING LISTENING AND SPEAKING

Collaborative discussion. Listening. Media literacy. Questioning. Reasoning. Building a speech. Performing a speech. Presentation literacy. Using digital media to support and enhance presentations. Adapting speech for audience and context. Looking back at Chapters 3–8, it's clear that assessing the complex skills they cover will be a daunting task.

Before we throw our hands up in despair, we need to remember that there is not one thing on the list that we wouldn't want students to master. We must remember also that we are not in this alone; no one teacher is responsible for ensuring that students master all this content. These skills should be taught across content areas and over multiple grade levels. Every class has listening and speaking components. Every teacher expects students to communicate, to listen, and to question. Every teacher should be involved in teaching and assessing these skills.

As I mentioned at the beginning of this book, it is not my intention to create a Common Core preparation manual. I use the standards as a template—a starting place for understanding and teaching the skills associated with strong listening and speaking. Likewise, it is not my intention to create a test preparation manual for the new Common Core assessments developed by the Partnership for Assessment of Readiness for College and Careers (PARCC) and the Smarter Balanced Assessment Consortium (SBAC). I will briefly discuss the format of these assessments, but my main focus will be more general advice for evaluating the skills the assessments attempt to measure. It's the kind of advice that will make it possible to teach students to exceed the benchmarks set on Common Core assessments as those tests evolve.

## Understanding PARCC/SBAC Assessments

Both PARCC and SBAC have the goal of creating standardized tests that states can use to verify that students are meeting the Common Core standards. At press time, 18 states plus the District of Columbia are part of the PARCC consortium, and 23 states plus the U.S. Virgin Islands are in the SBAC consortium. As you read this, numbers may have shifted, with some states joining and others possibly dropping out. Still, because the major education publishers are now tailoring their materials to align with new standards and assessments, the new PARCC and SBAC assessments will be affecting your students no matter what—even if you teach in a private school or in a state that has not signed on to the Common Core.

As schools across the United States are adjusting to the new standards, teachers are adjusting to the new assessments that will be replacing familiar ones. Like the standards themselves, the new assessments are designed to reflect 21st century learning—a new generation of assessments suited to testing the range of skills today's students need to master. While filling in answer bubbles is a perfectly good way to check vocabulary, knowledge of science facts, and ability to read for main ideas, it's a poor way to assess how well students can get information from diverse media or speak intelligently. However, digital tools easily support the evaluation of those skills and more.

Both consortia, as you are probably aware, plan to use computers for testing. Students will listen to audio or watch video and then respond. For this reason, students must be adept at getting information from audio and video sources. Additionally, the SBAC assessment has been designed to be computer adaptive: it will adjust as the students answer, basing the difficulty of each new question on the student's response to the previous one. We can argue the merits of continued high-stakes testing, of course, but at least the Common Core standards have pushed testing into the 21st century. Yes, access to the needed technology is still a potential roadblock, but rapid advancements are under way. While new tests may require more digital infrastructure than we currently have, they will push *us* into the 21st century as well and compel us to make important updates to our instruction.

## A Look at SBAC's Approach

Listening skills are embedded within the SBAC assessment. While some question sets are based on articles provided for students to read, others are based on audio students listen to or video presentations they watch. Students can replay the media if they wish. The questions may be simple multiple-choice items (selected response) or the more-involved constructed response (CR) type, challenging students to write sentences or fill out graphic organizers with key ideas. Primarily, SBAC assessment questions ask students to listen for the main idea and details. In the upper grades, the focus is on both listening and reasoning. In constructed responses, students identify main ideas, articulate the steps of procedure, and identify bias.

Listening will also be involved in some of SBAC's performance tasks. An 8th grade sample item requires students to read three articles and watch three videos before writing an argumentative essay about robot pets (listening, primarily, for main ideas as well as to get evidence for the essay). As designed, this performance would take 3 hours and 15 minutes: 60 minutes to read one article, watch two videos, and answer some short questions; 45 minutes to read the other article, watch the other video, and have a small-group discussion; and then 90 minutes to write the essay. It's a logistical challenge, to be sure. In theory, though, this performance task measures 8th graders' mastery of Standard 1 (collaborative discussion) and Standard 2 (analyzing information in diverse media). Other performance tasks have students create a speech for the purpose of assessing Standards 4, 5, and 6.

What's good about this approach is the inclusion of small-group discussion prior to the essay writing. It reflects how people actually develop understanding and work together to create a product (in this case, an essay). What's not so good about it is that it leaves certain skills included in the standards unaddressed. For example, Standard 2's focus on media literacy would support asking, "Why did the video's director choose this image or scene?" Standard 3 (questioning) would support asking students to consider higher-level questions such as, "How sound was the reasoning in Video 2?" The danger is that these skills' absence on the year-end assessment will encourage teachers to focus their efforts elsewhere.

## A Look at PARCC's Approach

PARCC envisions two modes of speaking and listening performance activities, one for students in grades 3, 5, 7, 9, and 11 and another for students in grades 4, 6, 8, and 10. Mode 1 performances, for the odd-numbered grades, will call for "real-time engagement" in listening and speaking. Students will listen to prerecorded speech or media productions and will spontaneously verbalize their responses to prompts. Mode 1 addresses Standards 2 and 3 (e.g., "analyze main ideas" and "delineate a speaker's argument"). Mode 2 performances, for the even-numbered grades, will require "advance preparation." Students will research grade-level topics and present a formal report to an audience. They will also be evaluated on how well they respond to audience questions after the presentation. Mode 2, then, covers Standard 4 (present information) and Standard 6 (adapt speech). These assessments will be teacher-scored, creating a challenge I will address later in this chapter.

## Assessing Listening

You may already have experience with one of the consortium-designed tests. In addition to the logistical issues is a more fundamental issue: *How do we evaluate the core skills?* If you have a recorded verbal response, how do you score it? How do you know your students are making progress, and what does success look like? Remember, I once thought my students were listening when they were still and quiet. A rubric based on my criteria would have been pretty unacceptable. Let's look at some ways to get a better picture of listening.

Yes, the rubrics used by SBAC and PARCC can provide a helpful starting place, but the easy availability of listening skill rubrics aligned with Common Core's Speaking and Listening standards doesn't mean we have to limit our evaluation to simply what's articulated in the standards for our grade level. We can ask for more. For example, Standard 2 implies that students should only be able to listen for information. Frankly, we will bore our students to death if we limit their listening to just informative texts. We can ask our students to listen to fiction and design listening rubrics for fiction, addressing skills like the ability to follow a story and the ability to analyze the motivation of characters in that story. We can have high expectations for listening comprehension even when enjoyment is the main focus.

## ➲ TAKE ACTION: Evaluating Listening

The goal of these activities is to help students (and teachers) understand expectations for skillful listening. Whereas my students might have said, "I *am* listening. I wasn't moving, and I didn't say a word!" activities that were more focused would have helped them (and me) realize better objectives. These activities are consistent with one of the main goals of this book—teaching these skills in a purposeful and specific way.

## Create and use a listening rubric (K–12)

SBAC has embedded item-specific rubrics into the ELA/Literacy Item Specifications available on its website. The same template SBAC uses as the basis for reading rubrics related to identifying central ideas and making inferences and conclusions might be adapted for evaluating listening tasks (see Figure 9.1). After all, both reading and listening share a key goal: getting information. Substitute the word "media" for SBAC's original "text," as I have done, and this rubric becomes a good starting place for various classroom listening assessments in that it focuses students on what to listen or look for.

Of course, in life we listen for many different purposes, and we want to teach and evaluate more than just informational listening. While skills like listening for the feelings a speaker is expressing or picking up on mood are trickier to assess, I encourage you to give students opportunities to practice them. Play around with this rubric's criteria and see what happens when you swap in new language of your own.

| Figure 9.1 | One Model for Listening Rubrics |
| --- | --- |
| 2 | A response:<br>• Gives sufficient evidence of the ability to justify interpretations of information<br>• Includes specific examples that make clear reference to the [media]<br>• Adequately supports examples with clearly relevant information from the [media] |
| 1 | A response:<br>• Gives limited evidence of the ability to justify interpretations of information<br>• Includes some examples that make clear reference to the [media]. Supports examples with limited information from the [media] |
| 0 | A response gets no credit if it provides no evidence of the ability to justify interpretations of information, includes no relevant information from the [media], or is vague. |

*Source:* Smarter Balanced Assessment Consortium, English Language Arts/Literacy Item Specifications, Smarter Reading Rubric Template for Short-Text Items, Claim 1, Targets 2/9 and Targets 4/11. Copyright 2014 by Smarter Balanced Assessment Consortium. Adapted with permission.

Try criteria like the following:

- Gives sufficient evidence of the ability to *understand the use of sound to influence message.*
- Includes specific references to *places where music changed to create feeling.*
- Adequately supports the *identification of sound use* with clearly relevant examples.

Remember that we want to measure "visual listening" also. Here's what that might look like:

- Gives sufficient evidence of *the ability to understand the importance of image selection.*
- Includes specific references to *images used.*
- Adequately supports the *identification of image selection bias* with relevant examples.

As we discussed in Chapter 4, it's essential that students listen (and view) with purpose. They need to know before a listening task what kind of listening they will need to do. Say that you have a task that will assess their ability to listen for the main idea and supporting details. Beforehand, tell students to focus on those aspects of a presentation or a video. Tell them to "block" their personal reactions to the message and ignore the soundtrack, if there is one. On the next viewing, give them the purpose of ignoring the main idea and focusing instead on image use or scene background. Adjust the rubric for each task.

The listening rubric you use should be shared with your students; the more familiar they are with how they will be evaluated, the better. Distribute or display the rubric when students are listening as you present information in class. Refer to the rubric after a student presentation, asking the class to write quick reaction papers while the rubric is on the screen. Select students to orally share written work, and let the class discuss how to score it. A cautionary note: there is a difference between a listening test and a memory test. Asking students to list the four main ideas or the three scene changes becomes a test of recall ability if you do not allow note-taking. Require students to be actively writing as they listen.

### Evaluate students' questioning ability (K–12)

The ability to ask pertinent questions is dependent upon effective listening. Typically, the way we check students' listening is to ask them for answers. This isn't enough—especially when we fall victim to Big Test Fever and find ourselves focused more on whether students can correctly answer a question that's going to be on a mandated assessment than on how effective their listening is.

After presenting information in class, try asking students to question the material rather than give answers. You might show an intriguing video and encourage them to write down as many questions as they can. Don't restrict the types of questions. Encourage both content-focused questions (e.g., "How many countries have universal health care?" is a very reasonable question for a civics class) and questions that relate to media literacy and message construction (e.g., "Why did the director use that camera angle?" "Didn't that soundtrack seem too dramatic?" "Why does this video have this title?"). Listen for evidence that they know how to ask for elaboration and how to tease out the speaker's motives. Give some prompts that demand questioning:

> *Teacher:* Here's what happened. She deposited the lingots on the parzivment. When he looked at them, he said, "All right. You have completed the requirements of the nalgend." Any questions?

There's no danger here that students will stay silent because they think they understand or don't know that they don't know. Try using this activity for formative assessment, checking to see how well students can ask questions to get clarification.

### Evaluate students' reasoning ability (4–12)

Reasoning is an essential listening skill, and if you wanted to, you could evaluate reasoning through standard kinds of testing:

1. What error is demonstrated in the following statement: *If you could think clearly, you would know that school lunches are bad for you.*

   a. circular reasoning

   b. attacking the person

   c. ignoring some facts

2. Fill in the blank with a statement that would make the argument true.

*All students want to learn.*

---

*Therefore, Karla wants to learn.*

However, reasoning is something that's best taught and assessed on an ongoing basis, not taught as a unit and assessed with a summative unit test. Every day, there will be some statement made in class that creates a chance to test students' ability to think logically and reasonably. An offhand comment can easily lead to an impromptu assignment:

*Simon:* We hate homework!

*Teacher:* OK, write a good argument to convince me I shouldn't give homework. You have five minutes. Go.

Look at the responses to see if students are demonstrating the "thinking backwards" we talked about in Chapter 5. Can they delineate the premises of an argument? In this case, not all of arguments need to be built the same way. One student may say, "All homework takes time. Students are busy outside of school and don't have time. Therefore homework must go." Another might say, "Homework can only be completed by students who understand the material. If you understand the material, you don't need more practice. Therefore, homework is unnecessary." Extend the activity by asking students to evaluate the arguments and assess the impressiveness of the premises. Which is most persuasive? Why?

## Assessing Speech Construction

In Chapter 6, we looked at the two distinct components of all oral communication: *building the speech* (all the things a speaker does before opening his or her mouth) and *performing the speech* (all the things a speaker does while speaking). Without that distinction, you'll never be able to accurately evaluate students' ability to do either one.

We'll start with speech construction. For the most part, the rubrics used to guide and evaluate student writing are also effective ways to guide and evaluate student *speech* writing. Whether a message is written or spoken, it must have good content and be well organized. All talks require a good beginning, a well-developed body, and an effective close. No, a speech is not "only an essay read aloud," but that shouldn't stop you from using a good score sheet for assessing writing to assess students' ability to craft oral communication.

In your rubric, you may want to emphasize only certain elements of speech construction. You may want to stress the need to include details, a piece of evidence for each point, effective transitions, relevant examples, or some other elements. Consider Figure 9.2, which shows a draft rubric that SBAC included in a sample performance task but has since abandoned.

| Figure 9.2 | A Somewhat Helpful Speech Construction Rubric |
|---|---|
| | **Use Evidence Rubric (Claim 4, Target 4)** |
| 2 | • The response gives sufficient evidence of the ability to cite evidence to support arguments and/or ideas |
| 1 | • The response gives limited evidence of the ability to cite evidence to support arguments and/or ideas |
| 0 | A response gets no credit if it provides no evidence of the ability to cite evidence to support arguments and/or ideas |

*Source:* From Smarter Balanced Assessment Consortium: DRAFT English Language Arts Item and Task Specifications, p. 26. Developed by Measured Progress/ETS Collaborative. Copyright 2012 by Smarter Balanced Assessment Consortium. Reprinted with permission.

This rubric example is a good reminder of a few rubric construction guidelines. First, try to avoid vague words. Where is the line between "limited" and "sufficient" evidence? These types of descriptors are what generate disagreement when teachers evaluate. They will become a problem as schools are asked to provide scores to the consortia for the locally scored listening and speaking items:

> *Evaluator A:* He cited one great fact that backed up his claim so I gave him a 2.

> *Evaluator B:* But he only had one fact, and I think three pieces of evidence are always needed, so I gave him a 1.

I also think terms like *limited* and *sufficient* offer little helpful guidance to students. Don't be afraid of numbers. For your assignments, be specific: "I'd like three pieces of evidence; one of these must be statistical and one must be an expert opinion." This avoids the problem of ambiguous language.

Recast this rubric to assess other components of content: "The speech gives sufficient evidence of the ability to provide reasons for every opinion" or "The speech gives sufficient evidence of the ability to provide opposing perspectives on an issue."

## Assessing Speech Performance

As I mentioned in Chapter 6, the Common Core's expectations for speech delivery are minimal. I regard them as insufficient requirements if the goal is to create speakers capable of impressing an audience. We can, and should, ask for more.

Consider Standard 4 at the 5th grade level:

> Report on a topic or text or present an opinion, sequencing ideas logically and using appropriate facts and relevant, descriptive details to support main ideas or themes; speak clearly at an understandable pace.

If you create a rubric using the multiple traits discussed in Chapter 6 (see p. 119), you will have a rubric that is aligned with both elements of the standard and includes all the performance components needed to be a successful oral communicator.

At press time, both SBAC and PARCC were developing speaking assessments. Perhaps they will require teachers to record students' speeches and send them out for scoring. Probably they will develop some speaking assessment that will be scored at the district level, with scores being "certified" by the district and then reported to the state. Audio and video recordings of student performances will be used for auditing those scores. The problem here is that teachers do not know how to evaluate speaking. In our classrooms, there are students speaking all the time, sometimes informally, sometimes formally. Sometimes we grade those speaking assignments. Now think about the rubrics and score sheets you use. How many of them are standardized? Do any two teachers in your building have the same idea of what it takes to be an effective speaker?

This leads to two difficulties. First, it means the scoring will be inconsistent. A student in one class might be scored "proficient" based on that teacher's rubric, yet the same speech might be "advanced" based on the rubric criteria of the teacher down the hall. Second, and more critically, this means the students will get inconsistent, sometimes contradictory, and often very wrong descriptors of effective speaking, which makes it difficult for students to piece together how to become competent communicators.

Here, too, is where we get into trouble if we fail to separate speech construction from speech performance and don't weigh the two components appropriately. Let's look at a common scenario. A teacher assigns an oral presentation. He hands out a score sheet in advance. Looking at the point totals, the students quickly see that how well they write is worth much more than how well they speak: the grade is based 75 percent on how well the message is written and 25 percent on "eye contact, enunciation, good pace, fluent delivery, and gestures." Because students get three times as many points for writing as they do for speaking, the teacher is essentially encouraging students to read a paper out loud; speaking well is very much a secondary concern. What the teacher has just done is set himself up to get an invalid assessment of speaking skill. Three examples will illustrate why.

- Speaker A writes a great essay (75 points). As he reads it, he wiggles and fidgets, which is fine because there is no score for that. Though he speaks monotonously, very quickly, and without gestures or eye contact, Speaker A pronounces words well and doesn't stumble over them. The teacher gives him 12 out of 25 points, for a combined score of 87. He is declared to be a "proficient speaker."

- Speaker B also writes a fine essay (75 points). While she delivers it, she is constantly flipping her hair out of her eyes and rocking back and forth, but according to the scoring guide, this is not a problem. She, too, speaks monotonously, uses minimal gestures, and doesn't make much eye contact, but her pronunciation is good, her words flow easily, and she speaks slowly. The teacher gives her 16 out of 25, for a combined 91: an "advanced speaker."

- Speaker C did not have a superior essay. The teacher noted a few grammatical errors in the text, good but not exceptional word choice, some disorganization, and a lack of detail, and awarded the essay 54 out of 75 points. As Speaker C talks, though, the class is amazed. He is poised and commands the stage. But this is not on the skill sheet. He is passionate, varies speeds for effect, has beautiful gestures, looks at each audience member, and speaks clearly as the words flow out of his mouth. He receives an enthusiastic 25 out of 25, for a combined score of 79. He is dubbed a "pre-proficient speaker."

All three speakers were scored incorrectly. If you were in the class listening, you would not have been impressed with Speaker A or Speaker B. You would have said, "Wow, Speaker C is really good!" I believe that when we score speakers, we should weigh performance *more* than preparation. I realize that few teachers would feel comfortable with that, partly because we have more experience teaching writing and partly because we feel it is somehow wrong to value style over substance. But I strongly disagree with giving three-fourths of the weight to the writing, as the teacher in my example did—and as a sample scoring guide for proficient speech that was drafted for and considered by SBAC did. Figure 9.3 shows an excerpt from that rubric, once available on the SBAC website.

What is really being measured here? Let's break it down.

"Establishment of Focus and Organization" is an obfuscating way of saying content and organization. The first column, "Focus," covers the content requirements: *include the main point* and *don't include extraneous material.* The second column, "Organization," is (obviously) an organization requirement, although you may wonder at the redundancy of stating both "employs a strong opening" and "effective introduction."

Moving on to "Development: Language and Elaboration of Evidence," the third column addresses another content requirement: *include support/evidence.* The fourth column pays lip service to audience, but it focuses on yet another content requirement: *use appropriate language.*

Here in the first four columns, we are measuring three elements of building a speech: *audience, content,* and *organization.* Another element of building a speech—presentation aids—slips in as the fifth column's final bullet. We could give a couple of presentation points for showing the media at the appropriate time, I suppose, but strong, appropriate, and effective visual, graphic, and audio enhancements are created well before the presentation. This means that even the one column ostensibly devoted to performing a speech is, in part, still about building a speech.

To make matters worse, the performance part of the speech, in addition to being seriously underweighted, does not adequately describe the elements of effective delivery. "Clearly" seems to suggest enunciation, which is redundantly echoed with "clear pronunciation." "Smoothly" is a common descriptor that actually conveys little to students. What does a smooth performer look like or sound like? The voice from your local smooth jazz radio station? A slick but low-key salesman? Is this term meant to suggest a mistake-free performance? No dropped note cards? No awkward pause because of a forgotten point? If we ask a student to act "smooth," what will we see?

| Figure 9.3 | A Misguided Rubric for Proficient Speech |
| --- | --- |

**Sample Generic 4-point Speech Rubric (Grades 3–11)**

| Score | Establishment of Focus and Organization | | Development: Language and Elaboration of Evidence | | Presentation |
| | Focus | Organization | Elaboration of Evidence | Language and Vocabulary | Presentation |
| --- | --- | --- | --- | --- | --- |
| 4 | The speech is consistency and purposefully focused:<br><br>• controlling idea, opinion, or claim is clearly stated and strongly maintained<br><br>• controlling idea, opinion or claim is introduced and communicated clearly within the context | The speech has a clear and effective organizational structure helping create unity and completeness:<br><br>• employs a strong opening and logical progression of ideas<br><br>• effective introduction and conclusion for audience and purpose | The speech provides thorough and convincing support/evidence for the writer's controlling idea, opinion, or claim that includes the effective use of sources, facts, and details:<br><br>• use of evidence from sources is smoothly integrated and relevant | The speech clearly and effectively expresses ideas:<br><br>• use of precise language (including academic and domain-specific language)<br><br>• consistent use of syntax and discourse appropriate to the audience and purpose | The speech is clearly and smoothly presented:<br><br>• use of effective eye contact and volume with clear pronunciation<br><br>• understandable pace adapted to the audience<br><br>• consistently aware of audience's engagement<br><br>• use of strong visual/graphics/audio enhancements when appropriate, to effectively clarify message |

The bullet points in column 5 may be intended to explain "clearly and smoothly." Speakers will be judged on eye contact, volume, pronunciation, and pace. Good! We recognize these as components of multiple-trait speaking with volume and pronunciation falling under the category *Voice* ("every word heard") and pace in the category *Speed.* No mention of *Poise,* though, which means there won't be points off for distracting behaviors. No mention of *Gestures;* no mention of *Life.* In short, only three of the six traits of effective oral communication are included—half of a good delivery. A lifeless recitation of a paper without hand, face, or body motions while gently (*smoothly*) swaying left and right will suffice. And that half is only worth 20 percent of the total score.

A rubric as poorly constructed as this one will lead to poor speakers being mislabeled as proficient. On one hand, that may lessen the anxiety associated with assessment, but we do no favors to students by failing to teach them how to communicate effectively. I do not recommend adopting the rubric in Figure 9.3 or anything similar to it, because it typifies the common mindset that speaking can be evaluated as if it were writing. SBAC has thankfully rejected that approach. You should, too.

## ◯ TAKE ACTION: Evaluating Speech Performance

Here are some things I *do* recommend—and I recommend them as the basis for a schoolwide initiative to let students know that being well spoken is important every day in every class. Students improve as communicators when we give them the message that all verbal activity matters, and when we give them the message that all educators are on the same page.

### Develop a consistent, schoolwide language to describe effective speaking (K–12)

When students move from grade to grade or from class to class, they should be able to expect the same evaluation system. You don't want one teacher scoring "articulation, content, and eye contact";

another scoring "elocution and projection"; another scoring "hold head up, speak slowly and loudly, good costume"; and so on. Remember to think hard about each word, as terms like *enthusiasm* are poor fits for serious or somber subjects. Make sure the words are simple and student-friendly; *elocution* might be "speak each word clearly." *Presence* might be "be poised." *Fluid body language* might be "use hand, face, and body gestures." My multiple-trait speaking model (PVLEGS) has been successful in schools. It transfers from young students to older students to adults. If you prefer to adopt other language for your school, keep it short and simple.

As part of that consistent language, make sure teachers separate "building a speech" elements from "performing a speech" elements on rubrics. The easiest way to do this is to design a rubric that physically separates the two. Devote the top half of the score sheet to audience, content, organization, visual aids, and appearance; devote the bottom half to *Poise, Voice, Life, Eye Contact, Gestures,* and *Speed.*

### Give equal weight to building and performing (K–12)

As discussed earlier, teachers overweight the preparation of the talk, especially content and organization. This gives students the erroneous belief that how well they present is of little importance. A speaking assessment must value the actual speaking. Your regular speaking assignments should be evaluated with 50 percent of the points linked to speech construction and 50 percent linked to speech performance.

A way to give students a sense of themselves as speakers is to at least occasionally provide assignments that value how well they talk *more* than how well they write. Assign a humorous speech about a funny life experience. The presentation could be done in person or via podcast. Do not score "main point, details, evidence" or "logical sequence." Instead, give most of the weight to *Voice, Life,* and *Speed,* which are important for a playful delivery. Assign a demonstration speech and heavily weight *Gestures.*

### Separate unlike descriptors (K–12)

Figure 9.4 is representative of many rubrics. This one was created to evaluate oral presentations about biomes. You may observe that the rubric evaluates writing conventions, including spelling. No one "hears" spelling. It is clear the authors took a writing rubric and tried to pretend it was a speaking rubric. If you recall the discussion in Chapter 6, you'll notice that two of the three speaking criteria are poorly worded—"loudly" and "slowly" mislead students. As you look closer, though, you may notice another problem.

What if a student completes work three days late and has only one or two examples of foreshadowing (a 1 rating) but has exceptional quality and a detailed illustration (a 4 rating)? Do you give her a 2 or 3, even though she had none of the descriptors in those categories? The mistake is to combine wildly different components in one numerical category.

Create separate scores for study skills (project on time); building skills (visual aids—detailed, neat illustrations; content—biome location, plants, animals) and performing skills (using PVLEGS). Students gain nothing from imprecise feedback and scanning a rubric to notice that they got one score from Row A, two from Row B, two from Row C, and one from Row D creates confusion ("So what's my grade?") rather than an opportunity for learning.

### Evaluate incidental speaking (K–12)

Our goal is to teach students to be effective oral communicators in all situations. To encourage improvement in one-on-one chats, small-group discussions, asking or answering questions in class, presenting solutions at the board, and other informal talks, evaluate students as they perform these tasks. Don't feel the need to do an evaluation of all of the elements of effective speaking each time. Select a day to focus on *Poise*, for example. Every time students speak, insist that they settle themselves, straighten up, stop fidgeting, and then talk. Give students the message that everyday verbal communications need to be well spoken.

| Figure 9.4 | Oral Presentation Rubric Combining Unlike Descriptors |
| --- | --- |

Name _____

Name of biome _____

## BIOME PROJECT RUBRIC

**4**     Completed on time

All sections carefully planned and neat; exceptional quality

Appropriate, detailed illustrations

Well-organized detailed summary of the biome location, plants, animals

Specific examples of animal and plant adaptations

No errors in spelling, punctuation, capitalization, and grammar

Always spoke loudly, clearly, and slowly

**3**     Completed one day late

Most sections carefully planned and neat; exceptional quality

Appropriate illustrations but with limited detail

Limited summary of the biome location, plants, animals

Limited examples of animal and plant adaptations

Few errors in spelling, punctuation, capitalization, and grammar

Mostly spoke loudly, clearly, and slowly

**2**     Completed two days late

Limited planning and neatness; minimal quality

Appropriate illustrations but no detail

Missing some key parts of biome location, plants, animals

Only one or two examples of animal and plant adaptations

Several errors in spelling, punctuation, capitalization, and grammar

Occasionally spoke loudly, clearly, and slowly

**1**     Completed three or more days late

Very limited planning and neatness; poor quality

Illustration missing

Missing most key parts of biome location, plants, animals

No examples of animal or plant adaptations

Many errors in spelling, punctuation, capitalization, and grammar

Did not speak loudly, clearly, or slowly

## Involve the audience in scoring (K–12)

A speech is for an audience. Most often, we ask students to sit passively as others talk or present. The only official evaluation comes from the teacher, and for this reason, students too often speak at the teacher, ignoring the rest of the audience. This is misguided. It misses the point of public speaking: communicating with an audience, not an individual. If a speech is given to an audience, only by asking for the audience opinion will we know if the speech was effective. Make sure students know they will be judged in part based on how well they communicated with the audience and that the audience will be involved in scoring (Palmer, 2011). Figure 9.5 shows a simple tool you can use to get the student audience involved.

Patty, a 4th grade teacher, prints this small score sheet six to a page, slices up the paper, and gives each student a handful of score sheets. At the end of each student speech, she gives students in the

| Figure 9.5 | Score Sheet for Student Evaluation of Peer Speech |

Your name _____

Presenter _____

| | | | | | |
|---|---|---|---|---|---|
| Poise | 5 | 4 | 3 | 2 | 1 |
| Voice | 5 | 4 | 3 | 2 | 1 |
| Life | 5 | 4 | 3 | 2 | 1 |
| Eye Contact | 5 | 4 | 3 | 2 | 1 |
| Gestures | 5 | 4 | 3 | 2 | 1 |
| Speed | 5 | 4 | 3 | 2 | 1 |

Comments _____

_____

_____

audience a minute to circle a number for each category (5 is high, 1 is low). She collects the scores, looks at them to verify that the classmates are recognizing the key components of effective oral communication, and then hands them to the speaker. Three means of formative assessment are in play here. The student gets feedback to help identify areas of relative strength and weakness; the teacher gets data about how well each student is progressing in impressing the audience; and the teacher gets data about how well the class understands the elements of performance. If a student never seems to improve scores in gestures, for example, he can be offered targeted follow-up with others needing help with that component. If the majority of the class gives scores in poise, for example, that differ from the teacher's own impressions, the teacher can reteach the concepts of poise.

Are students on the right track? For some reason, we have come to believe that the question can only be answered numerically. "Yes, students are on the right track, because on the last test, the class average was 74 percent, but now it is 87 percent." "Last semester, 42 percent were proficient or above, and now 56 percent are."

Sometimes numbers do tell the story. But sometimes, and we seem to have forgotten this, *teachers* can tell the story. Perhaps we cannot easily score how well students are reasoning, but we can sense when students are getting better. Maybe discussions are more on track and more fruitful, although we can't put a number on it. Perhaps we cannot exactly measure the growth in *Poise* and *Life,* but we can see the improvements. Maybe our video evidence shows students gave better presentations in the spring than they did in the fall.

Many of our evaluations of listening and speaking skills may fall into this non-numeric area. It is tempting to scoff at "I'll know it when I see it," but I am not opposed to teachers being allowed to use their judgment. Can you prove that your students are getting better at questioning? An acceptable answer ought to be, "Yes, I see it every day." But we can't see what we don't look for. Only by diligently looking for evidence that the students are making specific gains in the skills of listening and speaking will we be able to give students the guidance they need.

# FINAL THOUGHTS

Years ago, *Golf Digest* magazine announced a search for the worst avid golfer in the United States. To qualify, a golfer had to be between 35 and 55 years old, have no physical handicaps, play a minimum of 21 rounds of golf a year, and have a golf handicap of at least 36 (Andrews, 2008). The number of eligible golfers turned out to be huge: lots of people who spent a lot of time playing golf and yet remained absolutely terrible.

It is quite possible to get plenty of practice with a skill without getting good at it. I don't propose to start the search for the worst listener or the worst speaker in the country; I'm just pointing out that even though everyone reading these words has been listening and speaking for many years, it is the case that many of us are poor listeners, poor speakers, or both. It doesn't have to be that way for our students.

What an avid but awful golfer could do is find a competent professional and spend money on lessons. Over time and with the missing ingredient—consistent instruction—I bet every one of them would improve. In the same way, poor communicators will improve if they have competent instructors working with a consistent approach. Many golfers choose to continue playing without help, unconcerned about their dreadful scores. After all, it *is* only a game.

Students who sit in our classrooms every day and remain poor communicators aren't this way because of a choice they've made. Their situation is the result of educators' inattention to the critical skills of listening and speaking, and educators' indifference to developing the lessons students need to develop those skills. Unfortunately for students, this is *not* a game. Listening and speaking are absolutely critical to success—in school, in jobs, and in life. And every student would improve if we increased our commitment to teaching the core skills of effective oral communication. The activities we've looked at in this book are just the beginning. As you encounter others or create your own, I urge you to use them—and be sure to contact me so we can share them on my webpage. There are also entire books devoted to teaching effective questioning, media literacy, and excellent oral communication. I encourage you to explore those resources as well, as they complement and extend the ideas in my work.

As we have discussed, the Common Core State Standards movement has pushed educators to recognize the importance of listening and speaking. A new emphasis on college and career readiness means that skills that have been underserved for years are regaining a place in our schools. Like you, I have heard discussions about the appropriateness of some of these standards. "Preparation for *what* careers?" people might ask. "Does an aspiring electrician, retail manager, or firefighter need to be able to prove the subtraction formulas for sine, cosine, and tangent?" Perhaps not.

This much is certain, though: no student will ever say, "I don't see why I had to learn to discuss appropriately, listen well, analyze the barrage of information I receive, and speak effectively." It is a teacher's job and responsibility to assist every student in developing these essential core skills. Your students will thank you for taking on this challenge.

# REFERENCES

Anderson, C. (2010, December 27). TED curator Chris Anderson on crowd accelerated innovation [Video]. Retrieved August 1, 2013, from http://www.wired.com/magazine/2010/12/ff_tedvideos/

Andrews, P. (2008, March). The search for America's worst avid golfer. Retrieved August 20, 2012, from http://www.golfdigest.com/magazine/gd0585wagandrews

Bass, A. (2005). Enhancing listening skills. *The Balance Sheet.* Retrieved August 20, 2013, from http://balancesheet.swlearning.com/0905/0905c.html

Boyd, D. (2005). Wikipedia, academia and Siegenthaler [Blog post]. Retrieved September 18, 2013, from Apophenia at http://www.zephoria.org/thoughts/archives/2005/12/14/wikipedia_acade.html

Brookfield, S. P., & Preskill, S. (1999). *Discussion as a way of teaching: Tools and techniques for democratic classrooms.* San Francisco: Jossey-Bass.

Bumiller, E. (2010, April 26). We have met the enemy and he is PowerPoint. *New York Times.* Retrieved August 1, 2013, from http://www.nytimes.com/2010/04/27/world/27powerpoint.html?_r=0

Cain, S. (2012). *Quiet: The power of introverts in a world that can't stop talking.* New York: Crown Publishers.

Carr, N. (2011). *The shallows: What the Internet is doing to our brains.* New York: W.W. Norton & Co.

CAST. (2011). *Universal Design for Learning guidelines version 2.0.* Wakefield, MA: Author.

Common Core State Standards Initiative. (2010a). *Common Core State Standards for English language arts & literacy in history/social studies, science, and technical subjects.* Washington, DC: CCSSO & National Governors Association. Available: http://www.corestandards.org/ELA-Literacy.

Common Core State Standards Initiative. (2010b). *Common Core State Standards for English language arts & literacy in history/social studies, science, and technical subjects. Appendix A: Research supporting key elements of the standards, glossary of key terms.* Washington, DC: CCSSO & National Governors Association. Available: http://www.corestandards.org/assets/Appendix_A.pdf

Delpit, L. (2006). *Other people's children: Cultural conflict in the classroom.* New York: The New Press.

Education Northwest. (2013). About 6+1 Trait® Writing. Retrieved September 26, 2013, from http://educationnorthwest.org/resource/949

Edutopia Staff. (2012, December 15). *Five tips for building strong collaborative learning.* Retrieved February 26, 2013, from http://www.edutopia.org/stw-collaborative-learning-tips

Fall, R., Webb, N., & Chudowsky, N. (1997, August). *Group discussion and large-scale language arts assessment: Effects on students' comprehension* (CSE Technical Report 445). Washington, DC: U.S. Department of Education Office of Educational Research and Improvement.

Gagne, M. (2012, December 17). Tiverton Middle School group Skypes with authors to hear the stories' stories. *The Herald News.* Retrieved February 27, 2012, from http://www.heraldnews.com/news/x1631894112/Tiverton-Middle-School-group-Skypes-with-authors-to-hear-the-stories-stories

Hammond, D. W., & Nessel, D. D. (2011). *The comprehension experience: Engaging readers through effective inquiry and discussion.* Portsmouth, NH: Heinemann.

Himmele, W., & Himmele, P. (2012, December 6). Why read-alouds matter more in the age of the Common Core Standards. *ASCD Express, 8*(5). Retrieved July 31, 2013, from http://www.ascd.org/ascd-express/vol8/805-himmele.aspx

Krane, B. (2006). Researchers find kids need better online academic skills. Retrieved July 31, 2013, from *U. Conn Advance* at http://advance.uconn.edu/2006/061113/06111308.htm

Lent, R. (2012). *Overcoming textbook fatigue.* Alexandria, VA: ASCD.

Mackay, H. (2005). Now hear this! Good listeners have success. *The Times Union* [Albany, New York]. Retrieved February 20, 2013, from http://albarchive.merlinone.net/mweb/wmsql.wm.request?oneimage&imageid=6318133

Marzano, R. (2013, February). Asking questions at four different levels. *Educational Leadership, 70*(5), 76–77.

Mayer, R. (2009). *Multi-media learning.* New York: Cambridge University Press.

McMillan, D. (2010). *Life after death by PowerPoint 2010* [Video]. Available: http://www.youtube.com/watch?v=KbSPPFYxx3o

Measured Progress/ETS Collaborative. (2012a, February 28). *English language arts item specifications showcase 3 materials* [Draft]. Retrieved September 9, 2013, from http://www.acsa.org/MainMenuCategories/

ProfessionalLearning/OnlineTrainings/ACSAOnlinePD/Curriculum-and-Instruction-Leaders-Webinars/elaitems022812.aspx

Measured Progress/ETS Collaborative. (2012b, April 13). *Smarter Balanced Assessment Consortium: English language arts item and task specifications.* Retrieved September 9, 2013, from http://www.smarterbalanced.org/wordpress/wp-content/uploads/2012/05/TaskItemSpecifications/EnglishLanguageArtsLiteracy/ELARubrics.pdf

National Association of Colleges and Employers. (2012, October). *Job outlook 2013.* Bethlehem, PA: Author.

National Council on Disability. (2004). *Improving educational outcomes for students with disabilities.* Washington, DC: Author. Available: http://www.ncd.gov/publications/2004/Mar172004

National Education Association. (2012). Preparing 21st century students for a global society: An educator's guide to "the four Cs." Washington, DC: Author. Available: http://www.nea.org/assets/docs/A-Guide-to-Four-Cs.pdf

National Public Radio. (2010, January 13) Code switching: Are we all guilty? *Tell me more* [Podcast transcript]. Retrieved February 22, 2012, from http://www.npr.org/templates/story/story.php?storyId=122528515

Palmer, E. (2011). *Well spoken: Teaching speaking to all students.* Portland, ME: Stenhouse Publishers.

Palmer, E. (2012). *Digitally speaking: How to improve student presentations with technology.* Portland, ME: Stenhouse Publishers.

Pink, D. (2005, March). The book stops here. *Wired Magazine, 13*(3). Available: http://www.wired.com/wired/archive/13.03/wiki.html

ProCon.org. (2014). *About us.* Available: http://www.procon.org/about-us.php.

Reynolds, G. (2008) *Presentation Zen: Simple ideas on presentation design and delivery.* Berkeley, CA: New Riders.

Rubenstein, G. (2008) *Collaboration generation: Teaching and learning for a new age.* Retrieved January 16, 2013, from http://www.edutopia.org/collaboration-age

Schwerdt, G., & Wupperman, A. (2011, Summer). Sage on the stage. *EducationNext, 11*(3). Retrieved March 4, 2013, from http://educationnext.org/sage-on-the-stage/

Shaw, T. (2008). *Integrating listening, reading, writing, and speaking skills in the foreign language classroom to increase student proficiency and self-perception of proficiency.* Retrieved January 29, 2013, from http://digitalcollections.carrollu.edu/cdm/singleitem/collection/edthesis/id/30/rec/16

Shrum, J. L., & Glisan, E. W. (2000). *Teacher's handbook: Contextualized language instruction.* Boston: Heinle & Heinle.

Sticht, T. G., & James, J. H. (1984). Listening and reading. In P. D. Pearson, R. Barr, M. L. Kamil, & P. Mosenthal (Eds.), *Handbook of reading research: Volume I* (pp. 293–317). White Plains, NY: Longman.

Treasure, J. (2011, July). *5 ways to listen better* [Video]. Retrieved August 9, 2012, from http://www.ted.com/talks/julian_treasure_5_ways_to_listen_better.html

Walsh Dolan, M. (1985). Integrating listening, speaking, reading, and writing in the classroom. *Language Arts Journal of Michigan, 1*(1), 4. Available: http://scholarworks.gvsu.edu/lajm/vol1/iss1/4/

Weaver, C. (1980). *Psycholinguistics and reading: From process to practice.* Cambridge, MA: Winthrop.

Wikipedia. (n.d.a). *Wikipedia: About.* Retrieved August 20, 2013, from http://en.wikipedia.org/wiki/Wikipedia:About

Wikipedia. (n.d.b). *Reliability of Wikipedia.* Retrieved September 18, 2013, from http://en.wikipedia.org/wiki/Reliability_of_Wikipedia

Worth, R. (2004). *Career skills library: Communication skills* (2nd ed.). New York: Ferguson.

Zapato, L. (2013). *Help save the endangered Pacific Northwest tree octopus from extinction.* Retrieved January 16, 2013, from http://www.zapatopi.net/treeoctopus/

Zinsser, W. (1988). *Writing to learn.* New York: Harper & Row.

# INDEX

# ABOUT THE AUTHOR

**Erik Palmer** is a professional speaker and educational consultant from Denver, Colorado, whose passion for speaking has been part of every one of his careers. Before going into education, he was the national sales leader for a prominent commodity brokerage firm, a floor trader on a Chicago commodity exchange, and a founder of a publicly traded commodity investment firm. He left the business world and became a teacher, spending 21 years in the classroom in the Cherry Creek School District in Englewood, Colorado, primarily as an English teacher but also as a teacher of math, science, and civics.

Erik is the author of *Well Spoken: Teaching Speaking to All Students* and *Digitally Speaking: How to Improve Student Presentations with Technology* and a program consultant for Houghton Mifflin Harcourt's English Language Arts program, *Collections*. He presents frequently at national, regional, and state conferences, and he has given keynotes and led in-service training in school districts across the United States and Mexico focused on showing teachers how to improve students' oral communication and help develop the skills necessary to speak well in school and beyond.

Erik can be reached through his website, www.erikpalmer.net, or the website he has devoted to oral communication, www.pvlegs. com.

## Related ASCD Resources

At the time of publication, the following ASCD resources were available (ASCD stock numbers appear in parentheses). For up-to-date information about ASCD resources, go to www.ascd.org. You can search the complete archives of *Educational Leadership* at http://www.ascd.org/el.

### ASCD EDge Group

Exchange ideas and connect with other educators interested in English and language arts, Common Core State Standards, and 21st century learning on the social networking site ASCD EDge™ at http://ascdedge.ascd.org/

### Online Courses

Common Core and Literacy Strategies: English Language Arts (#PD11OC135)

Common Core and Literacy Strategies: History/Social Studies (#PD11OC132)

Common Core and Literacy Strategies: Science (#PD11OC133)

### Print Products

*Common Core Standards for Elementary Grades K–2 Math and English Language Arts: A Quick-Start Guide* (#11314) by Amber Evenson, Monette McIver, Susan Ryan, and Amitra Schwols; edited by John Kendall

*Common Core Standards for Elementary Grades 3–5 Math and English Language Arts: A Quick-Start Guide* (#113015) by Amber Evenson, Monette McIver, Susan Ryan, and Amitra Schwols; edited by John Kendall

*Common Core Standards for Middle School English Language Arts: A Quick-Start Guide* (#113012) by Susan Ryan and Dana Frazee; edited by John Kendall

*Common Core Standards for High School English Language Arts: A Quick-Start Guide* (#113010) by Susan Ryan & Dana Frazee; edited by John Kendall

*Engaging Minds in English Language Arts Classrooms: The Surprising Power of Joy* (#113021) by Mary Jo Fresch, Michael F. Opitz, and Michael P. Ford

*Teaching 21st Century Skills: An ASCD Action Tool* (#111021) by Sue Z. Beers

*Teaching Reading in the Content Areas: If Not Me, Then Who?* (3rd Ed.) (#112024) by Vicki Urquhart and Dana Frazee

For more information: send e-mail to member@ascd.org; call 1-800-933-2723 or 703-578-9600, press 2; send a fax to 703-575-5400; or write to Information Services, ASCD, 1703 N. Beauregard St., Alexandria, VA 22311-1714 USA.